Leaderpreneur

Leaderpreneur

A Leadership Guide for Startups and Entrepreneurs

Aaron Vick

CONTENTS

1. Chapter One: Entrepreneurship and Leadership — 6
2. Chapter Two: Business Startup — 26
3. Chapter Three: Vitalizing Your Business — 41
4. Chapter Four: Management Through Leadership — 58
5. Chapter Five: Advancement Via Leadership — 71
6. Chapter Six: Effective Pipeline Management — 78
7. Chapter Seven: Administration & Leadership — 92
8. Chapter Eight: Relationship Building — 104
9. Chapter Nine: Economic Affairs — 117
10. Chapter Ten: Augmentation — 136

11 Conclusion 154

Copyright © 2020 by Aaron Vick

Leaderpreneur
A Leadership Guide for Startups and Entrepreneurs

All rights reserved. This book remains the copyrighted property of the author. It may not be reproduced, copied, stored in a retrieval system, recorded, scanned, and/or distributed in any manner for commercial or non-commercial purposes without the express written permission of the publisher or author, except in the case of brief quotations embodied in critical articles or reviews.

Publisher Information
ISBN 978-1-7356780-1-6 *Paperback*
978-1-7356780-0-9 *Ebook*
Edited by E. Lee Caleca

Disclaimer

All the information in this document is for informational and educational purposes only. The author assumes no responsibility for any results that stem from the use of the information herein. While conscious and creative attempts have been made to ensure that all information provided is as accurate and useful as possible at the time of the writing, the author is not legally bound to be responsible for any damage or loss of income caused by the accuracy as well as the use/misuse of this information.

Introduction

"Entrepreneurs succeed not just by creating a good product or an innovative company, but also by developing themselves into leaders."
~Madanmohan Rao

Many entrepreneurs have been frustrated out of their endeavors because they could not figure out the element they were missing, the one that might lead to success in the venture of their choosing. They were not acting as leaders. They had not developed those skills.

Leadership plays a pivotal role in all business platforms. So many entrepreneurs assume all they need is the skill and ability to think of a brilliant business idea, build a pitch deck that presents the idea as ingenious and, in turn, sells itself.

However, this pattern of thinking more often than not leads to a failed business startup. For success with any startup, you have to have more than an idea; you need *drive*, a *plan*, and *execution*.

If you've been struggling with getting your business off the ground or if you simply have an entrepreneurial vision, then you have picked the correct book to guide you throughout your venture.

This book is a staple for all entrepreneurs, most specifically budding ones, to educate and provide advice that has lead to successful business models in a plethora of different sectors.

You may be currently wondering if entrepreneurship and leadership go hand in hand. The answer is... sometimes. Someone can be a leader without being an entrepreneur, and an entrepreneurial spirit might only get you so far without leadership skills. These roles are related and interchangeable in a countless number of ways!

Without question, any business that manages to run successfully without the element of clean and concise leadership merely is just running on the fumes of LUCK.

Any successful entrepreneur will tell you they did not start (and find lasting success) with their business by brainstorming and creativity alone; they began by leading and taking on responsibilities wherever and whenever needed.

This book is a treasure trove of insight regarding general traits a leader must have, and the ones shared by accomplished entrepreneurs.

However, before you dive in, you need to prepare your mind for the journey. I hope that this book changes your entrepreneurial mindset & alters your approach to business effectively and efficiently.

As you read, you might need to release some of your previously held beliefs and prior tactics you have used in the past to try and achieve your goals. The very ideology and techniques you are currently utilizing may very well be the things hindering your successful startup.

You must be open to suggestions and ready to heed advice from those who have already forged their paths to prosperity, or you will simply find yourself spinning your wheels, unable to reach the destination to which you are aspiring.

Ultimately, there is a reason you chose this book. If you decide to use the information to your benefit, a successful business startup is within your reach, but only if you heed the advice of the experts meticulously.

If you desire to procure knowledge about leadership centered startups, how to set up your ideal business and maintain it, or you simply want to be enlightened to the world of startup leadership, you have taken the first step forward!

Are you ready?

Chapter One: Entrepreneurship and Leadership

Let's start off with a few foundational elements. It's essential to define and discuss the terms and concepts we will encounter along the way.

So many love to refer to themselves as entrepreneurs, but few truly grasp what the title entails. The ability to be smart and skillful when it comes to business does not automatically categorize you as an entrepreneur.

Similarly, many people refer to themselves as leaders just because they have found themselves in positions that allow them to oversee and direct others. This thought process undermines what it means to be an effective leader, a task that takes intricacy, and the proper skill set per the role.

Leaders are diverse in responsibilities, functionalities, and personalities. Leadership is a melting pot of a wide range of ingredients that must be measured precisely and used as directed.

The following information should begin a self-dialogue that allows you to examine and expand upon what qualities and strategies form successful entrepreneurs and leaders, and the principles of the business world.

You will be cultivating a mindset toward business that will propel you toward prosperity in your endeavors.

Who is an Entrepreneur?

There are several contradicting definitions of the term entrepreneur, all of which are correct. Some people take the position that an entrepreneur is an individual who runs or owns a business and bears the responsibility of financial risk. Others may claim that an entrepreneur is an individual who manages and organizes an enterprise.

These definitions are only textbook. They take a broad stance regarding entrepreneurship but that's not all there is about being an entrepreneur.

There are some essential characteristics that should never be left out when defining an entrepreneur.

Entrepreneurs have a variety of characteristics and personality traits that separate them from the average individual. They have the innate ability to think critically and uniquely. It is not uncommon for them to exhibit risk-taking behaviors and nonconformist methods to reach targets. Generally speaking, entrepreneurs stand as a master to none and practice superiority and leadership in all facets of their business.

Consequently, it is not mere words or definitions that catapult these individuals toward success, but instincts and approaches to business that are innovative.

Traits of an Entrepreneur

There's no time like the present for assessing, reassessing, and growing a skillset. This is always at the forefront of my mind.

Being a part of numerous startups and working within corporate teams (while being an introvert) has provided me with an abundance of curiosity around how we interact. Watching and not participating is for the young mind.

As you begin to see various interactions, you also see opportunities to insert yourself, your knowledge, and your abilities, which will provide you purpose.

One of the abilities I believe exists in all of us is *leadership* to some degree. But most people are not concerned with leading so those skills are never explored. Though it may be true, some are born leaders, this should not discourage the rest of us from learning and leading.

Leading is much more than commanding the troops or standing at the podium demanding people should listen because you have the ultimate authority.

Leadership is about serving, it's about strategizing the needs of the whole and the individual. Also, it's about strategizing the internal and external factors that keep a team, a department, or a company intact.

In 2020, we were faced with a global pandemic caused by the rapid spread of COVID-19 (a.k.a. the coronavirus). The virus reached the majority of the world's population in weeks causing severe breathing conditions in many and a horrific number of deaths.

As I wrote this book, there were still people sheltering inside their homes as first responders, medical staff, and grocery, fast food, and other essential service workers acted courageously to keep the world afloat.

The pandemic sparked my curiosity into leading. It's something that can be done from any position you may hold but now anyone can harness leadership for good.

Additionally, the CEO of my company and long time friend Billy Hyatt, was activated by the Army Reserves to lead a COVID-19 Response Team in a city where the virus was creating an epicenter. (There have been many epicenters since the outbreak, causing some cities to run out of hospital beds and important medical equipment to help the very sick breathe).

The top executive position in our company defaulted to me via the succession plan in place. As a new CEO, I had to migrate the entire company to 'Work From Home' status, held many company-wide Zoom Social Hours, transition an R&D project into a full SaaS launch, and jump into the company lead during the start of a global pandemic!

Whew!

I am now looking at the future of the company as the pandemic maintains a tight grip on the world economy.

The immediate challenges seemed to appear from nowhere. It was not easy, still isn't easy, and I haven't learned it all. The stress of taking on the role of CEO amidst the very shaky future of the global economy was heavy.

Failure was a real option.

However, these challenges forced me to continue learning how to be a better leader, a better listener, and hopefully a better servant. The decisions I made then (and still today) were rooted in the reliance of gut and, more importantly, confidence in my growth as a leader and entrepreneur.

Here are some traits you may possess that can be useful to becoming a successful entrepreneur and leader:

1. **INNOVATION**

    Individuals with wild businesses are known to be real entrepreneurs. They are always on the hunt for exclusive business opportunities. Every new idea they have will always have the hallmarks that display electrifying cravings for being at the zenith of *business artists*.

    Seasoned entrepreneurs understand that every situation and event is a potential business opportunity. They constantly generate ideas about efficiency, workflows, people skills, and promising new businesses. They have an aptitude for observing their environment, and for utilizing and maximizing everything they find to attain their goals. They are creative people. They have solutions to problems and also repurpose dormant things to their advantage.

2. **PASSION**

    Passion is one of the essential traits of successful entrepreneurs. They sincerely love their work to the point of it being a passion too. They are enthusiastic and willing to dedicate extra hours to secure the success of their business because of the joy they get from their business surpasses the money. Successful entrepreneurs always read and research methods for making their business better.

    A true entrepreneur wants to see what the view looks like and how things work at the peak of every business mountain. The minute they see and observe it, all they want to do is to go further and further to attain it. They get driven by the passion and never allow failure or speedbumps to stop them. Yes, they can slow down and they could fail, but they are not quitters.

3. **RISK TAKING**
   If anyone wants to be a successful entrepreneur, they must be a believer in the harsh reality that things can go south.

   A successful entrepreneur always has a success story that is out of the box. They will take you through the tales of losses, setbacks, and so many other 'misfortunes' they passed through until they got their big break!

   The point is that they never stopped!

   One could even call a successful entrepreneur a gambler!

4. **LEADERSHIP**
   Leadership is the key. No successful entrepreneur can tell you they never had to take control of things--people, situations, and circumstances--on the way to the top.

   Entrepreneurs, even though they are gifted with diverse degrees of flair and charm, are also potential leaders. Having the same level of enthusiasm for a new religious convert, they motivate other people to be part of their mission.

   Delightfully brave, these thrill-seekers recruit team members and followers who are sometimes even smarter and shrewder than themselves.

5. SURVIVAL INSTINCT

The survival instinct is another important one to have as an entrepreneur. True entrepreneurs are not always caught unaware by circumstances. Instead of them accepting defeat in the face of obstacles, they immediately dig deep and employ one of the other characteristics for which they are famous--optimism.

Every day is a new day for true entrepreneurs; it's a fresh opportunity to develop and realize their vision. They believe change is constant and erratic, and their team or followers also develop that mindset. That's how they thrive.

In summary, a true entrepreneur is an individual who can build, sustain, as well as perpetually renew their various businesses, with a mastered skill of balancing risk-taking, self-reliance with prudence, hard work, trusting staff, and delegating authority.

The list of all the characteristics of an entrepreneur does not end here.

There are some other traits you should watch out for, such as discipline, confidence, open-mindedness, independence, competitiveness, creativity, optimism, determination, strong people skills, and a strong work ethic.

If you have all these traits all wrapped in your personality, then congrats; you are a true entrepreneur. If not, don't fret and keep reading!

Who is a Leader?

"Leaders are innovative, entrepreneurial, and future-oriented. They focus on getting the job done."
~Brian Tracy

In almost every setting in the world, be it religious, social, business, academic, and so on, there is always a leader, a ranking system whereby an individual or a set of people are rated higher than the others. We'll be discussing the business kind of leadership.

Leaders play a very vital role in any organization. The decisions they make and the actions they take affect the whole organization. The fate of the followers and the organization rests in the hands of the leader.

Some people inherit leadership positions, such as those born into royal families for example. Or, as with me when I was unexpectedly thrown into the role of CEO during a pandemic!

However, being born into a leadership role does not make someone a good leader. As an entrepreneur, you may not naturally have the traits of a leader, but the exciting part is that leadership can also be learned!

I can tell you from my personal journey that the skills I have today were learned through watching others who I admire as leaders, lots of reading, and just giving it a go. Sometimes you have to learn a bit through trial by fire.

I digress, back to the skills of leadership.

Entrepreneurs need to possess leadership skills in order to establish, inspire, and stimulate highly productive teams on a long-term basis.

Self-knowledge and self-awareness are the groundwork of the entrepreneurial leader skillset. You'll discover that most of the qualities of a leader can also be found in a successful entrepreneur: resilience, flexibility, passion, motivating skills, trust, and focus; they are all mutually inclusive.

Traits of an Entrepreneurial Leader

"What is admirable about entrepreneurial leaders is that they have an insatiable hunger to keep going to the next level."
~ Shaima Hamidaddin

Let us discuss some traits of the entrepreneurial leader to help bring awareness of what will be helpful through your personal journey.

1. **COMMUNICATIVE**
    As a leader, you should have the ability to articulate your ideas in language that your team understands, as well as the strategy to accomplish common goals. A true leader encourages communication among all departments and levels in an organization.

    Everyone has a voice and everyone is right, but it's your job as a leader to successfully relate why one idea might be more effective to the task than another.
    In other words, feelings matter, particularly when you're dealing with creatives. Your people need to feel as though they are contributing to the team, as though they themselves matter.

2. **VISIONARY**
    Successful leaderpreneurs have clear visions. They know precisely where they want to go and how to get there. They share

their vision with the team, communicating the big picture inspirationally, working with them diligently and flexibly so that together, as a team, the company can realize that vision.

3. **SUPPORTIVE**

    Entrepreneurial leaders understand the significance of supporting the team. Here are a few items that may help assist with fostering a supportive environment:

- *Initiative*: allowing and encouraging team members to think outside the box and to follow through with their ideas
- *Reactiveness*: allowing team members to use their own creative expression rather than trying to control their inventiveness
- *Dynamism*: allowing ideas to flow organically and encouraging vigorous activity leading to exciting and dramatic innovation.

Therefore, they do everything they can to motivate and provide the *support* needed by the team to attain their goals.

4. **SELF-CONFIDENCE**

Self-confidence is a common and shared trait among both leaders and entrepreneurs. An entrepreneurial leader must have a great belief and trust in their ability to implement, direct, and successfully realize their vision.

Confidence must also be built from experiences over the years: the failures, setbacks, feats, and lessons that have honed the entrepreneurial spirit. A true leader is conscious of their strengths as well as his weaknesses. They demonstrate their skills without arrogance.

5. **SHARE SUCCESSES**

Leaders celebrate with their team whenever a milestone is accomplished. They humble themselves enough not to take credit for everything or hog the limelight.   They recognize the input of other team members and share the accolades accordingly.

Apart from all these qualities of an entrepreneurial leader, there are other vital traits one must possess before one can master entrepreneurial leadership skills.

- **Involvement** - A good leader must be involved in virtually every activity that happens in the organization. As your company grows, this may not be something that can be overseen by just one person, which is when you begin to build your management team. Some of the day-to-day decisions should be delegated so you can focus on larger and longer-term items.

- **Nurture** - A good leader must create a conducive atmosphere that enhances growth for the team and the organization. No one wants to work under an iron fist or in complete chaos as a culture will break down, morale deteriorates, and turn over will be high.

- **Transparency** - A good leader must be honest in every area. Honest entrepreneurial leaders quickly earn their employees' trust and respect.

- **Perseverance** - A good leader must be willing to go the distance.

- **Decisiveness** - A good leader must keep learning and be open-minded, weighing plans, goals, and ideas fairly then acting upon the evidence for the best outcome.

You have to digest and embody all these traits if you ever want to join the team of successful leaderpreneurs.

Now, let's move on to discuss the principles applied in the business world.

Rules of the Jungle (The Business World)

Even with the perfect business ideas, tactics, and execution procedures, if you do not understand the principles that guide every business, then you may find it challenging to secure a successful startup. Many people have tried to start up a business without following these rules, and they end up failing.

Here are a few things you should know before diving into any business:

1) PROFIT IS MORE IMPORTANT THAN ANYTHING ELSE

In business, it does not matter how large your organization is; it is useless if it does not yield any financial return. Even if you are making a lot of impact on people or other businesses, not making profits will ensure you cannot operate the business for long. Even if you are a pre-money company seeking venture capital, at some point, there will need to be a path to monetization.

A good friend of mine always says "Profit is King"!

2) OFFER VALUE

"You can get anything you want in life by helping others get what they want."
~ Zig Ziglar

Do your search for successful businesses out there like Google, Twitter, Facebook, and Apple, and you will discover a movement of value offering.

If you genuinely want to set up your business successfully, start thinking about what value can be offered. What pressing issues can your company solve? Can you innovate an existing product and make your product or idea more desirable than the next guy's?

Always be looking to answer the "WHY" when starting a business as it will be the driver for customers making a purchase. Why should someone buy from you? Why do they need your product or service? Why are you a better choice for them over the next guy?

3) YOU NEED MONEY TO GROW

It takes money to make money.

This old adage has stood the test of time because it's true. But do not misunderstand its meaning.

There are several case studies out there about thriving businesses that began from zero; but most startups require some funding along the way. At some point, be prepared to reach a stage when you have no other option than to invest your personal money or the net cash earned from sales into the business; not doing so would suppress your growth.

4) MAKE THE RIGHT ACQUAINTANCES

It's not what you know but who you know. Sound familiar? This is another old adage that applies very well in business. There is so little that can be achieved on your own.

You'll eventually need other people in order to move forward.

These people might be business associates, advisers, employees, mentors, partners, and so on. Just ensure you always have the appropriate people in your circle. This will grant you access to the various resources, information, advice, encouragement, support, and networks you need to succeed.

Don't be afraid to reach out for help--even if it's just a virtual coffee--to ask a mentor some questions or establish an advisory board for keeping your tech in-line with the needs of the customers.

5) NEVER STOP LEARNING

This is an essential trait of an entrepreneur, as discussed earlier.

Knowledge is Power.

If you maintain a persistent stance to never change, in spite of any argument in favor of change or innovation, your business will begin to die immediately.

This does not apply to branding, where your brand remains the central identifying mark of your business. What it applies to is the constantly changing world we live in--to those things you are not aware of that are happening outside your immediate world. When you start to become close-minded and rigid, with a narrow outlook, you are hamstringing your efforts and the creative efforts of your team.

The 2020 COVID-19 global pandemic is a great example of how learning and adapting is critical for businesses to thrive or make it through hard times.

Many businesses, especially consumer retail, were forced to close the doors and create spaces that adapted to social distancing measures and routine cleaning procedures. Other businesses, like mine, had to act fast to cut costs, manage client fears, and create new operational protocols literally overnight.

Businesses tend to move a bit slower when it comes to overhauling existing processes even if they are not the best implementation. Sometimes it's to save money and others require extensive planning and coordination due to complex system
connectivity.

However, because of the pandemic, many businesses both public and private had to expedite long term development plans as well as make adjustments to business development methods, customer interactions, etc. These sweeping adjustments had to be fast-tracked leading to a massive compression of implementation timelines.

All-in-all, the global spread of COVID-19 led to organizations rushing to make adaptations to the new normal within months.

I personally cannot think of another time since WWII where the majority of the world had to adapt to the current events vs. plan for the future over time. Maybe a future book will be centered around the impressive feats companies accomplished within 3 months of a global pandemic when the typical timelines would have been 3 years!

On to number 6...

6) VISUALIZE

Ensure you know your prospects and your market fit.
Think through questions such as:

- What is it you want to achieve?
- What portion of the market do you want to reach, change, or enhance?
- How will you get to that position?
- What will it take?

This does not mean you must have a robust business plan from the outset (though you will need one eventually); however, these strategic questions help visualize and reveal the big picture--the potential end result.

7) EXECUTE

I do not mean you should begin to chop off people's heads. Be someone who executes quickly after collecting enough data to make an informed decision. Someone who gets fresh and ideal ideas acquires new knowledge and executes all viable courses of action immediately.

There are a lot of people out there with potential business ideas, but they won't make any difference in the world if they're not taken to the execution phase. This is a critical skill and should not be underestimated in your plan for business advancement.

According to *Harvard Business Review*, "this was ranked first in importance on a list of sixteen skills" senior managers look for in their team, and it applies doubly to you as an entrepreneurial leader.

But it's also important to be clear and methodical in your execution so you don't burn out or lose team members. Plan, assemble resources, organize your people, and make sure to connect what you and they are doing to the strategy of your business.

8) MARKET AND SELL

If you do not promote your business or fail to sell yourself out there, then you are just going to join the set of entrepreneurs who failed to successfully grow their
businesses.

Great business ideas cannot stand alone; they do not count here. Many successful companies did not make it just because they produce attractive and useful things, but because they are very skilled at marketing their brand. (For example, the cosmetics industry often spends up to forty percent of their advertising budget on designing effective packaging.

Why?

Because it's the perception of beauty--the implication that this product can help someone achieve the beauty implied by the packaging--that sells these products.

9) BE TENACIOUS

Establishing a new business is not easy. The chances for failure on your first attempt are quite high.

You may have countless competitors out there, against whom you must measure your company's product or service.

Competiton does not mean you should give up or not even try; it means you have to be tough, determined, and dedicated to finding your niche, given that you strongly believe in your business idea.

Be persistent and consistent!

Remember that persistence generally comes with more reward than talent or genius!

10) BE FLEXIBLE

Never be too rigid in your plan.

It is not healthy for you or your business to run at the same pace all the time or not be able to make adjustments. *Take heed*: not being flexible can make you go bankrupt either monetarily, physically, and/or mentally.

Be open-minded about what is working and what is not, and drop your ego and pride. There's no place for either in business.

Be always ready to acclimate your business framework and make necessary changes for the survival of the original idea. If you thought it was a good one to begin with, it's worth pursuing until the data says otherwise.

Set goals within your plan that help you and your team achieve objectives. Set deadlines. When we know we need to accomplish something within a certain timeframe, we tend to become more focused on the task. But if a deadline is missed, learn why and just keep moving forward.

Cultivating the Right Mindset towards Business

This section is a short summary that concludes our discussion for Chapter One: Entrepreneurship and Leadership.

Carefully observe the ten rules below about cultivating the right mindset towards business. They will go a long way to steadying your business skills on a long-term basis.

1. Always try out new things, challenge yourself, and *be persistent*.
2. Always be open-minded about learning new things. Get a mentor, if possible.
3. Always regard failure as another means or opportunity to learn. Every failure should be considered an experiential success.
4. Always keep a record of your successes. (This will work to keep you motivated when you're feeling discouraged.)
5. Always surround yourself with gifted and talented individuals who believe in your vision.
6. Always find time to cool off. Get rid of stressors.
7. Create routines for yourself and be dedicated to them.
8. Set goals that are attainable and time-conscious.
9. Always allow your instincts to direct you.
10. Ensure you are determined enough to not become complacent in your business.

Now that you've learned the basics of being a leaderpreneur let's dive right into the business world--how you can start up your own business, and how to be productive.

Chapter Two: Business Startup

The inception of any business should begin with setting the foundation!

An ancient Turkish proverb says, "A building without a foundation is soon demolished." An English proverb backs that up by saying, "No good building without a good foundation."

These sayings emphasize the importance of a good foundation for any building, likewise a business, which can be likened to a structure.

The successful launch of the business relies on the foundation upon which it's built, hence the necessity of paying adequate attention to this.

Success hinges on a good startup, as to how you begin determines a lot in terms of the growth and progress of the enterprise.

Now you know this! So, in this chapter, I will be taking you through business startup steps (the inception) and how to set up a business or enterprise properly.

I am sure you have an idea of what a startup is, but let us begin by understanding what the concept of "business startup" actually means and what it entails.

A business startup refers to the establishment of an entity or the starting point of a company. Business startup also means the beginning or early stage, especially in its development.

From the conception of a business idea to the formation of the company, how do you ensure you are on the right track, setting the necessary foundation for your business?

Preplanning a Business Idea (Building Your Blueprint)

This is when you fully develop your business idea and set out plans for the implementation of those ideas. It is when you set up a blueprint to follow to bring your idea to life. This is a very important aspect of a startup.

It is the period when the idea is mapped out. Your blueprint is your design plan; it is the roadmap of what you want to create. Thus it is vital to be as detailed and intentional as possible.

The more time you take with this--the more detail and life you can give it and the clearer your vision--the better your chances of successfully implementing it.

At this stage, try to analyze every aspect of your business idea to ensure that the concept is developed correctly. When you look at the finished blueprint or plan, you should be able to see a clear vision about what you have.

For example, if the idea you are nurturing involves the production of products, your plan should include its specific nature, an analyzation of your intended market (gender, age, demographic), needs and resources (where to purchase the raw materials, the materials of choice, your projection of how much you will initially need, costs, and so on).

Endeavor to cover every detail.

A detailed plan is a better plan. The purpose of covering every aspect is to ensure that you know what you want. When you can see it in writing, you can make changes and adjust accordingly, and you can more easily figure out a plan to achieve it, the second step in the startup plan.

This is the stage where you will hopefully spot any potential obstacles. For example, by knowing the kind of material you want to use in the production of your products, you can research the best places to get those materials. If some laws or factors might hinder getting those materials, you can figure a way around it before you get to that point.

It makes more sense to know upfront that there might be some law that will prevent you from purchasing a large quantity of certain metals, for example, so you can work around that and possibly find some alternative material. It will be far less costly to tackle it before you get into the business itself.

Continuing with the product-based business, there may also need to be considerations to on-demand product creation versus bulk manufacturing. Initial funding for engineering and costs to create prototypes and samples could require more time and attention once you begin to flesh out the product.

The same holds true for software development. While an idea builds excitement and sparks your initial drive to succeed, keep in mind that the next step of moving an idea to tangible assets is tough, critical, and stressful.

Many new businesses fail because potential issues were ignored at an early stage. You might not, however, always know the answer to every single area of production, as some things will be discovered as you go, but you should endeavor to uncover as many issues as possible.

Here are some tips to help keep you on track.

1) Plan to build a company you believe in.

Not every good idea is going to be something you can fully get behind and believe in. If you're not sure--completely sure--that you can follow through with an idea, your doubt will affect your belief in the capacity of that idea and you're ability to grow it.

Don't decide to give it a go anyway just to see how far you can get. This is not the best approach. The first investor in your business is yourself. If you cannot convince yourself that your idea and plan for the business is good enough, you won't be able to convince others. Your strength and conviction will waver and eventually fall apart, along with the enterprise. Except for the fact that you'll have gained some experience, you'll just be wasting your time.

Passion is one of the greatest strengths you can have for the business you want to bring to life. It is the fuel that will keep you going during the darkest days when everything seems to be going wrong, funds are low, morale is low, and you're wondering whether you should simply quit.

You will encounter obstacles that will make you want to give up, but your belief in the fact that your idea is a winning idea--your passion for it--will give you the strength to try again--to keep going. So, make sure you believe 110% in your business idea.

2) Do not be afraid to be different.

Originality and innovation are major selling points in business. If your new and different approach is you being creative and original--you are on the right track.

Do your research and find ways to make your business--your product, software, or service--stand out. Build on existing market problems. Dive in and try another approach to finding a solution to a problem.

3) Business is a marathon, not a sprint.

You have to be in for a long haul. You have to be ready to be patient with the process. Most good things don't happen overnight.

You have to willing to dedicate time to the grind and give your business time to grow before turning in the kind of profit margin that pushed you into it in the first place.

So, it is necessary to be very realistic with your goals for the business. An excellent way to test yourself for the readiness to run your business live is to *double the time and cost and half the sales* then check to see if you can survive. Let your answer guide your actions. This is preparing you for the worst situations that can arise from the reality of running a business.

Implementing Your Business Idea

> *"Ideas are useless unless used. The proof of their value is in their implementation. Until then, they are in limbo."*
> **- Theodore Levitt**

This quote points out the importance of implementing your idea. This is when the real business starts. After adequately following the pre-planning guidelines, the next stage is putting every part of the idea into implementation--in the proper order of course.

Ideas alone do not make a business, but the implementation and execution of those ideas do! Therefore, it is essential to take your ideas from the drawing board to the market.

During the implementation phase, some things may not go according to plan. If you set up some guidelines to work by before you begin implementing your idea, they will help you get back on track. But, remember to stay flexible. Every plan has potential weak spots, but if you know this ahead of time, you can roll with them and adjust your course of action.

1) **Do not over-compromise.**

It is expected that some aspects of your idea may not be feasible. Ideas are thoughts with unlimited possibilities, but when it comes to actual implementation, your idea must stand the test of reality. Some things just won't work and you'll need to figure out a way to compromise.

Compromise is not wrong or a bad idea, but be careful not to compromise the core idea. Certain products or services can be tweaked to meet market requirements or customers' needs; however, the core values of your business should not be compromised, only the means and approach you take to fulfill them.

Every business has fundamental values in which it was established. These basically include your mission statement--what you stand for. These values guide the running of the business and the kind of products and services offered.

These values should never be compromised as they are in line with the vision and purpose of the business. They are the guiding principles of your business and should always be used to keep the business in check.

These values are not the same as your idea or who you think is your target customer base. Sometimes there is a need to re-assess, make adjustments to the product, and/or pivot. This is not the same as your values.

At Cicayda, I registered a trademark for iDiscovery®. Discovery is a particular phase within the litigation timeline where our core services were offered. Our core values were culminated in that registered term to include a dedication to people, technology, and innovation.

iDiscovery® embodied the focal points we thought were critical to our success and to ensuring our clients were given the most comprehensive approach to their problems. These values did not change even as our software product lines evolved so we could adapt to our technologically advancing market.

Think through the core values for your startup. Maybe it's a dedication to providing the best value to customers, a smarter way to manage data, or never wavering on
quality.

2) Try to do more with less.

Outside of you--the founder and visionary--money is the lifeblood of your company. Try to do the most using as little capital and resources as possible. Try to achieve your goals with a minimal budget. Control spending in order to extend the lifespan of the business.

Runway is extremely important for a startup to monitor. Any funds dedicated to a startup are part of the runway whether it's cash from your savings, family & friends donating to the cause, or VC investment. The total amount of funds divided by the total monthly expenses will provide the number of months you have to make it work before additional capital calls or revenue is required to keep the doors open.

Be very economical about the budget and runway, because sustainability is the ultimate goal of the company; this does not mean quality should then be compromised. Make moves like buying in bulk, buying from the closest retailer to the wholesaler, etc. There is always a route to cutting down costs; follow that route.

When you're creating your budget, provide for miscellaneous items (generally at least 10% of your overall product development budget) to give space for any little fine-tuning that may be made, whether it's in the price of goods, unexpected needs, or additions needed to make the plan viable due to adjustments. Make sure you always do the most possible with the least money.

3) Keep money aside in case of mistakes.

No one ever intends to make mistakes, but mistakes are inevitable; they cannot always be avoided, which makes it necessary to make provisions for errors.

Certain kinds of pressure can make you abandon your vision or produce a toxic working environment, and one of those stressors is monetary pressure.

Certain mistakes will require you to adjust your plan, which may cost you time and money above your original assessment, so having money kept aside to accommodate for this halts any pressure or fear that might arise from these mistakes.

Not all mistakes can be corrected or recovered. However, their effects can be minimized, so having funds dedicated to this will act as a confidence booster.

The bottom line is this: keep spending under control as much as possible.

4) Create a lasting brand.

Always keep in mind the importance of building a sustainable brand and let that thought guide your actions.

The goal of creating a lasting brand will keep you from making certain kinds of decisions, especially those that would put the trust in the brand into question.

Your brand should be the guiding factor in terms of customer interaction and product quality. Any decision that does not comply with your vision & mission statement about what you want your brand to represent--what you want your company to stand for--should be seriously reconsidered.

I know, branding sounds like something you should not be worried about since branding seems to be reserved for big names like Apple, Coke, Google, and Disney.

However, branding can also be effective within the circles YOU operate.

Are you a brick & mortar store? Then maybe the branding you are looking for is purely based on a set geographical area.

Are you a niche software for a specialized industry? Then maybe branding for you is centered around the industry connections and conference circuit.

The above guidelines are born out of experience and research. Allow them to keep you in check when creating your blueprint, building your plan, and implementing your business idea.

The Role of Leadership in Startups

Leadership is a required skill for starting up a business. You will need to take charge of every situation in the beginning and handle problems as swiftly as possible.

At the startup, you would also be in charge of whoever is working to put your products together, build your software, or helping to carry out the service you offer. All of these areas need a demonstration of your leadership skills.

Do you feel you do not possess essential leadership skills in business relations? Keep calm; I've got you. I will share some secrets to becoming a great leader for your business.

Firstly, you have to note that this is *your business*.

YOU are the front line of things in general. You are also in charge of and responsible for the goals you want your business to accomplish, both now and in the long run, so you need to take charge literally.

Do not just claim to be the brain behind the startup idea in name only. Good leadership is not gauged simply by what you know, but by how you handle situations, including people & relationships, negotiations & disputes, errors & timelines, and everything else that can potentially occur.

Start by setting clear goals for the business; this would serve as direction for you and everyone on your team giving you and your employees a clear picture of what to work towards.

Set both short-term and long-term goals so so everyone knows what's expected of them, and everyone can feel good about accomplishing something with each completed task.

Of course, these goals will hinge on your vision for the business. To ensure adequate performance, it is necessary to bring employees in on the goals of the company. Share your big picture visions for the business so employees understand where the business is headed and will work in accordance. Do it from the place of leadership. You will gain the trust and cooperation of your employees. Also, set the right examples. As a leader, the best way to teach is through your actions.

Your actions act as a yardstick to determine what is right or wrong in terms of the business. so it is essential to leave the right trail. Instead of continually yelling and telling them what you expect, make yourself a proper example of what you expect from them and watch them try their best to act in accordance.

Learn to articulate your thoughts properly.

(This is easier said than done for me!) I will also note this is the single most difficult part of leading for me. I suspect for many reading it may be the most difficult as well; especially if you have a tendency to be introverted and/or are somewhere on the Spectrum. Stay persistent, know you won't get it right all the time, but that only means you have to strive harder to be your best.

To be a good leader, you want to pass a message or voice out an opinion with confidence--a critical leadership trait--speaking clearly and loudly, making sure everyone can hear you, This leads to excellent communication between you and your team. It is essential to always communicate with your employees and view them as team members.

By properly communicating with your employees, you pass a message that they are essential to the business, and you value their opinions. This gesture goes a long way to positively affecting their attitude towards work and gives you various perspectives to consider.

Ask questions, a voice out complaints about their work or state of things, involve them in various problems and ask them for their solutions. Allow everyone to have a voice, and also praise them when they do things right. Give credit where credit is due. When the business achieves some commendable goals, appreciate the efforts of the employees, and give a special shout out to those who partook in whatever led to achieving the goal. Give the team certain perks if you can afford to and watch how it boosts their performance.

By appreciating the efforts of the employees to getting things done, it gives them the feeling of relevance and importance to the progress of the company, and this is a work boost for them. It increased their motivation to work harder and their input to the success of the business. It also exalts you as a humble leader who does not always take all the credit.

Adequate communication helps to foster a peaceful and cooperative working environment as well as an open floor for more ideas and solutions to problems.

As the head of a business, you stand as the main decision-maker. Being a good decision maker makes you a good leader. Be ready to make a decision in those harsh and awkward moments and try to be firm and confident in the process. This presents you as a good leader.

Finally, when things go wrong, do not pass the blame, take responsibility when you are wrong, and make sure to learn from those mistakes. Bouncing back from mistakes, handling mistakes, and taking constructive criticisms are signs that would uphold you as a good leader.

Need a second opinion? Go listen to Big Sean's "Bounce Back" and then come back. I'll wait.

Your Mission and Vision

The mission and vision of your business revolve around the core values you have set up. You have to be as intentional as possible with these values as they are the foundational purpose of the business.

Every business shares a common goal of optimizing profit-making, but besides that, what other values propel your business? What values drive the company and direct the actions of everyone who works for the business?
Defining these items is what the mission and vision are meant for. They are a healthy blend of what your company represents and the goals the company aims to achieve.

Don't start a business without first exploring a vision and mission statement.

At Cicayda, we defined our value proposition via iDiscovery®: the combination of people, technology, and innovation. This bled into our vision and mission statements.

A vision statement refers to an account or sentence which highlights the objectives of the company and guides business decisions to align with its values and set goals. They are future-based goals meant to inspire everyone who works in the startup.

A mission statement on the other hand describes what the business currently is--why the company exists, the kind of business it is (in terms of the goods or service it offers), and states the goal of its daily operation.

These mission and vision statements are a good reminder of what you are as a business venture, where you currently are, and where you are heading to. They also do well to highlight the business goals and values which guide the actions of those who work in the business venture or organization.

They act as a constant reminder and a source of motivation and inspiration, and every worker needs that. Before you hire anyone, make sure they are fully on board and believe in your vision and mission.

Cicayda's Mission Statement:
We empower clients by combining technology with the personal touch of express in order to minimize risks, costs, and poor outcomes for corporate legal departments and law firms.

On the part of the customers, it gives them an overview of the business and brings them in on the sort of the goals to be achieved. This way, they feel like a part of the bigger picture. Note that our mission is client-focused based on what we believe our core values are.

It is advisable to have the mission and vision statements printed and pasted in a public part of the organization where both workers and customers can see them.

The four-plan approach discussed in this chapter should guide you during the startup (inception) of your business.

Chapter Three: Vitalizing Your Business

Growth! This is the desire behind any kind of business, and between you and me, growing a business is not as easy as it sounds. However, in this chapter, we will explore a way to handle this guaranteed roadblock on your path to success.

Linear Growth vs. Scaling Your Business

The first secret is figuring the type of increase you seek out for your business--how you want it to increase--as there are two different methods; growing your business and scaling your business. Follow on and understand the difference and come back to thank me for this secret.

In a growth plan, you add resources to the business--money, people, technology--in order to increase revenue. Generally, the amount of new resources you add should be equal to the amount of new revenue you want to see.

Increase your revenue by adding equal resources or input to facilitate that increase. That is, the business is gaining more revenue on the ground of equal added value of input and resources. Hence, the profits and losses are evened out.

Just in case you are still confused, in simpler terms, it is gaining $30,000 in new revenue after investing $25,000 worth of resources or input (or both). Thereby, this revenue increase is premeditated.

Scaling a business, on the other hand, involves building up a company to enable growth with little or no involvement. That is, setting your business up to allow it to get more revenue faster than it takes on more cost. Simply put, scaling your startup sets up your business to gain $30,000 in terms of revenue after spending just $5,000, for example.

Scaling a business can be a better option; the difference between growing and scaling a business lies in the setup.

Scaling your business involves patronizing wiser input and cost schemes to maximize revenue. Growing your business also uses appropriate input and resources schemes, but they are not aimed to over maximize the revenue possible.

Growing is more about linear expansion.

A typical example of how these two different concepts work is this: If a business gets a deal which requires you to hire more hands or requires a certain skill set, in order to make this new deal work-- to grow the business--you will hire more staff with the required skillset. This intake would require more cost which, after the revenue derived from the new deal comes in, matches or almost matches that revenue.

In the same scenario, scaling the business to meet the needs of the new deal would involve hiring contract staff or freelance staff for the newly required skill set. They come on board just for that deal and require less outlay in terms of cost (no insurance, no paid sick days, or holidays). This ensures that they are not a static economic increase. When that deal or project is completed, they are out. In this way, subsequent revenue does not get evened out by the cost of input and revenue from previous deals.

Other ways to scale may be to build your software to autoscale as the needs of clients grow so you are not shelling out capital to "grow" or wait for the business to grow.

Now that you have seen what both concepts are, I assume you'll scale your business, so let us learn more tricks on how to scale your business and establish an amazing growth pattern fully.

To vitalize your business in the present-day world, there are **four areas** to look out for to maximize the success potential of your business.

These areas are:

1) INTERNET.

The world of today cannot be described without using the term *internet*. The internet, since its emergence, has dramatically changed the world and the way we conduct business, especially the pattern of communication.

Knowing fully well that the internet is here to stay, it is imperative to join the train. You should not even consider conducting your business without it.

Websites have largely replaced business cards. If your business does not have an online presence, people who shop electronically will simply go elsewhere. The market is on the internet; you have access to global international markets to buy and sell anything, and this increases the number of your potential customers. And most importantly, this is not going to change.

Most millennials and younger shop online, and the next generation will know almost no other way to shop. It's what they were raised on as the norm, not a nice-to-have.

Online is where you'll find a large potential customer base, and it is necessary to understand how they shop, search, and research so you can access these customers with the intention of adding revenue/sales/users.

The most important first step to accessing the internet market is to build an effective, user-friendly, interactive website. (Some have moved to embedded pages such as Facebook business pages, but that functionality is something you do not own nor have full control over. A domain and website is a small corner of the worldwide web you can call your own.)

Websites have become necessities of businesses in the world today. You will need to claim a spot, build and furnish the site, then let people know you're there.

Here are some fundamental marketing tips to pay attention to in terms of the creation of your company and brand website.

- **GIVE DETAILS.** Let your website tell the story of your business: It is of utmost importance that your website explains what your business is all about. That means the goods or services you offer must be evident in every aspect of your website. You cannot be selling furniture, for example, without adding images and descriptions of your inventory. Everything should be there: prices, fabric content, dimensions, colors, options, and so on.

- **BE USER FRIENDLY.** Ensure your website is easy to navigate. Opt for simpler designs that are easy to navigate and comprehend by consumers. Use tabs to categorize whatever you offer. They should be expandable, drop-down menus that are easy to notice--either at the top of the page or in a sidebar.

  The website should be navigable from all devices. One of the issues with electronic viewing is that people like to increase image or font size; they turn their phones sideways, screens are different sizes (desktops, laptops, cellphones, tablets), even with the same category (15", 17", and so on). This means your site should have both mobile and desktop versions with full responsive user interface.

- **CONTENT.** The content of your website is an essential component of both the site and your business. It should directly reflect what you are and should include an **"About Us"** page that summarizes the story of your business and the value you offer, a **"Contact"** page that contains the accurate information on how customers can reach you.

- **IMAGES.** Add images of actual products or images of your service in action with real people/users illustrating its use. A detailed description of the goods or services you offer is also helpful.

  Have attractive pictures taken that are in keeping with the overall theme of your site and your brand. The web requires certain DPI or high-resolution photos. If you're not experienced in this, hire a professional.

- **WRITTEN CONTENT.** The same goes for written content. Hire a professional to write content, or at the very least, to proofread it. If someone is on the fence about purchasing from you, typos and misprints and blurry images can send them to someone else. If everything on your site is professional and attractive, it represents the fact that your business is professional as well.

- **BLOG.** The word 'blog' is a truncation of 'weblog'. This is where you can discuss topics relevant to the line of business you are in or explain ways that the products or services you offer can be used.

Remember to use easy-to-read fonts in writing your content. Many people think using fancy fonts or varying fonts throughout the site makes it look more creative. Not so. People will experience difficulty reading. Which brings us to the next vital characteristic of building a website: Consistency.

- **CONSISTENCY.** Your pages need to be consistent through the site. Choose a theme first that represents your product or service, then design your page background. This is the background you will use throughout, for each and every page. Keep fonts and image size consistent, with the exception of your banner.

Website development is much easier than it used to be thanks to thousands of template choices for platforms like WordPress as well as other out-of-the-box solutions such as Squarespace and Wix.

2) SOCIAL MEDIA.

This modern phenomenon is also an essential path to growing your business. There are various social media platforms you can utilize to market your business, including Instagram, Facebook, LinkedIn, Twitter, TikTok, and so on.

It is vital to pick the one(s) which best suits your line of business and proceed to indulge your customers.

If your startup has a business-to-business (B2B) focus, then LinkedIn may be the right choice.

If you run the regular buying and selling, Instagram and Facebook are good choices. If you offer services, you may add Twitter to the platforms you use as a way to engage, connect, and inform customers.

On these platforms, endeavor to project your business and whatever value you provide in the best light. Post content that will appeal to your customers, and they can engage with in terms of comments and replies.

Just remember that if you start using social media, you must be consistent and social!

Why are followers that engage important?

The whole idea of social media is that information is passed on to others, so the more followers your company has (& the more they interact), the larger the potential to gain even more people/followers, all of whom will be potential customers/purchasers.

Keep your posts brief and relevant. Offer sale or event information, new trends, personal stories, or anything else that is relevant to what you're company is doing right now. Spark a debate or run a poll. Get a conversation going instead of just promoting.

Using one or more social media platforms is a good way to grow your business, but again, once you start, you must follow through. You must respond to comments and questions in a timely fashion. It's advisable to hire a professional community manager or social media manager to help with this.

Keep in mind, you can go overboard with social media platforms, so take the time to identify the correct platforms for your business.

3) **YOUTUBE.** YouTube is a platform for visual content. It is an excellent place to demonstrate how to use the products you sell, or speak on the services you render, or advertise those services by carrying out examples. Again, these videos should be made by a professional.

4) **GUEST POSTS.** This involves finding popular websites that relate to your niche and allowing guest writers to post pre-approved and vetted content on your site. Or you can do the opposite: write quality content on the goods and services you offer and post them on other relevant sites. Either way, the article is then linked back to the writer's site.

The internet is the present, so it is highly necessary to key in. Just in case you are still debating on the use of the internet to grow your business, remember the majority of the world's population use It, so do not let your business be forgotten or undiscovered. Renew the relevance and availability of your business in the sight of your clients by regular and consistent uploading of compelling content.

5) **NETWORKING.** Networking involves making contacts and exchanging information with specific people to develop a relationship that would be mutually beneficial to both parties. Both parties, however,

have a common interest or line of profession. Networking does not stop at exchanging information but further involves trying to maintain long-term relationships by utilizing or referring as many of your network business contacts as often as possible, and the people in your network will do the same for you and your business.

Networking is crucial in growing your business because:

- **It gives you an avenue to exchange ideas.** Like a famous quote says, "no man is an island," networking exposes you to varying views from people in similar fields, and these ideas can help in growing your business. Knowledge is attributed to a pool of information and networking exposes you to this pool of information.

- **It brings about publicity.** Being in business means you need to be seen and known, and networking can help get you there. By meeting people and establishing a good relationship with them, these people further introduce you to other relevant people and this way you are gaining publicity from the people who matter. You cannot become known by keeping to yourself.

- **It brings about new opportunities.** One of the significant objectives of networking is the opportunities it exposes you too. From establishing relationships with relevant parties, when opportunities come up, your name can come up. It is essential to have people who advocate and bargain for you in your absence, especially in the face of opportunities. That is one of the biggest benefits of networking.

- **It helps with necessary support.:** As a businessperson, you will regularly seek to indulge in new ventures, and sometimes you need assistance in terms of finances, contact, and other ways.

Networking helps you meet the people who might be inclined to give you the support you seek. Especially when you network to the right people, these people can be of relevant help and support when needed. They subsequently help grow your status.

Now you know the benefits of networking, how do you network? How do you encounter opportunities to network?

- **Join a business-oriented group.** Associations are a coming together of like-minded people--people with similar interests-- and most business networks have the goal of growing member businesses through network contacts.

Choose a group you feel comfortable with, and have your 30-second and
60-second speech practiced and ready. You must be able to tell people in 30-60 seconds the basic points of your business.

Have business cards ready with your name, business name, website, and contact information. When people give you their cards, jot down some bullet points on the back of the card about your conversation with them to refresh your memory, and follow through within 24 hours with a quick email telling them you enjoyed meeting them and look forward to mutual benefit.

- **Attend relevant business seminars and events.** There is no better place to network than a gathering of business-oriented individuals. By attending business events and workshops, you have a double win. The first win is by gaining whatever knowledge is shared at the event; the second win is the opportunity to network and rub minds with bright business individuals.

- **Get involved with community events and situations.** This might not scream a win, except you know the benefit of delayed gratification. As a business owner, an excellent way to gain the attention of other high-meaning individuals is to help in a community cause.

    Ask yourself questions like how can your business help out and aid in a particular situation--whatever the cause is for the event, charity, or community endeavor. Though this is not a profit-making idea, it is a good publicity and networking idea.

    Your business comes to the attention of relevant individuals and possible individuals you may not have thought could help your business.

    You can also sponsor a community event, putting your business in the forefront. If you do this, be sure to have an access table--somewhere at the event where high-meaning individuals can speak to you. This makes it easier to access high-meaning individuals who take part in the event (sponsor perks).

Now onto marketing!

Marketing

Marketing refers to the activities taken in a bid to promote and encourage the purchase of goods and services. It is the promotion and advertisement of products and services. Marketing is an essential part of growing your business as it creates brand awareness and encourages sales, which subsequently increases revenue.

In the past, marketing strategies for business used to involve creating branded merchandise and obtaining information from customers, but times have changed.

Presently, the internet plays a significant role in the marketing of businesses. So currently, what are the best marketing strategies to grow your business?

- **The internet:** As earlier stated, it is essential to leverage the use of the internet in present-day marketing strategies as that is the newest, most useful, and productive way to reach many at one time.

  In the preceding paragraphs of this chapter, we talked about the internet and how to use it to grow your business; those means are also part of the best tricks to market your business.

- **Use of email marketing:** Email marketing is merely marketing via emails. It involves sending emails of the product description and available products to customers and potential customers on your email list.

  Once your customers agree to receive your exclusive emails, then you can advertise to them this way. The email marketing software also keeps a record and helps you figure out tactics that are working and relevant to your subscribers.

  Many utilities are available for email marketing. Some are embedded within their Customer Relationship Management platforms like Hubspot. Other workflows may be cobbled together for maintaining lists and connecting them to your email system such as MailChimp.

There isn't a one-size-fits-all approach and you may opt to start with one method then switch to another depending on your funding and internal resources.

- **Use of influencer marketing:** This is also a subset of the internet as the influencers use the internet to run the advertisements. Influencer marketing involves the use of people who are knowledgeable in a particular area and have a measure in that field to grow your business.

You send them products or access which they review or create content around and make them open to their usually large following.

Influncers are not only helpful with physical products. Even with software
platforms there are ways to build your audience and encourage fans to become influencers.

Most recently, I was fortunate enough to watch the startup Fast (Twitter: @Fast) begin to prepare for their launch of the software. Their social media presence was on fire and began to show how engagement online vs dumping information out to the ether provided a very large network of interested users. In turn, the users began to interact, share, and promote a service that had not even launched.

Kudos to the @Fast team and I encourage you to follow them (and me, of course) on Twitter:
@Fast
@domm
@mkobach
@aaronvick (me, but I'm just a Fast fan!)

- **The use of SEO and SEM:** SEO refers to search engine optimization, which involves the use of relevant keywords and metrics to ensure your content from your business website or blog ranks high and is easily discoverable when that keyword is searched.

  SEM or search engine marketing, on the other hand, refers to a marketing practice that involves paid advertisements above the search engine results of a keyword.

  Both Search Engine Optimization (SEO) and Search Engine Marketing (SEM) are fundamental aspects of present-day marketing strategy. In helping to grow your business, if you know how to navigate through these strategies correctly, they are useful forms of advertising that will subsequently increase revenue.

- **Affiliate marketing:** This is another present-day marketing strategy. It involves the use of affiliates who are usually individuals who would refer people to purchase products or services from you and, in turn, get commissions on every sale they propelled.

Again, this outlet has been predominately focused on physical product-centric
selling. However, there are ways to make this work for other items like

software through similar partnerships with folks like AppSumo or ProductHunt.

The various marketing strategies discussed need to be correctly understood before indulged in as they are quite complicated to work around. However, once you have a good understanding of how each of them works, they are fantastic strategies to grow your business.

- **Domination Competition**: As the name implies, it involves dominating your competition.

And how do you go about this?

Firstly you have to know your competition. Knowing who your competitors are is necessary to devise strategies to remain on top.

Dominating comes in all shapes and sizes. You may be able to "dominate" your market by carving out a niche, making something better than what's already out there, or you just have something that is different. Embrace it and go tell the world.

Some principles to use to dominate your competitors include:

- **Fill the gaps:** Check your industry; pricing, type of goods, availability, or whatever it is, and try to fill any gaps in those areas. Leverage on the void to be filled. You can examine the needs of the customers in your industry and try to meet those needs.

- **Outspend your competition with social currency:** There is always an area that your competitor currently dominates, maybe in their choice of ads. Look for a similar functional area and outspend there. For example, if your competitor is already dominating with the use of search engine marketing ads on Google, then you use social media and find the best forms of ads to run there--maybe use influencer marketing and dominate with that.

- **Create experiences for your customers:** How? By making your products or service more indulging or easier. For example, if you sell a product, you might want to invest in your ambiance; this way, when customers come to purchase goods, they enjoy the benefits of a pleasant ambiance.

  Take pictures and videos to post on your website, and that way, your business is on the lips of people. Ask customers for help by posting on social media with a hashtag and a photo. There are also ways to easily implement video testimonials to your website that can be shared across social media and on your website.
  Side note: If you have both a brick and mortar store and an online store, both should be coordinated in terms of appearance and ambiance: colors, style, theme, and so on.

- **Have excellent knowledge of your target audience:** Study your target audience and their market behavior and find out ways to improve their market experience. Knowledge never goes wrong; it helps you figure out when, where, and how to come in.

These are some ways to get above others in your industry. Remember, even when you are leading, you cannot be relaxed as changes can occur anytime, and you have to be prepared for whatever market turnaround occurs. Stay flexible and keep tracking your marketing results.

- **Heading your business**: Yes, be a leader! As the head of your startup, the scaling of your business largely lies in your hands.

Try to do adequate research as that is the only way to figure out what areas of your business need to be grown and the approach to take to ensure the growth.

If you want something adequately done, do it yourself. So, make sure you are involved in every aspect of the business, and you lead in every area. You have to delegate tasks but still make sure you supervise the work done to ensure nothing leaves your notice.

The various means of scaling your business may look like the essential points you hear everywhere, but remember the success of an approach is not in knowing the path but in execution.

Read and put into practice the different points raised in this chapter.

Make relevant changes and get in control of the situation; remember you are a leader!

Chapter Four: Management Through Leadership

The success and growth of an institution, business, or startup are usually the things referred to when an individual is talking about the management of an institution.

In most of these situations, people usually believe that management is in the hands of the employees rather than the employer. They claim that the success, independence, and growth of a particular business relies on employees and their ability to work collectively in a team, that is, teamwork. However, this is not only a few of the factors that contribute to the success of a business.

In addition to teamwork, the leadership, skills, and plans set in place for the business are also huge contributors.

The most important of these is the contribution of the leader, simply because excellent and stable leadership would ensure that everything else, such as proper planning, falls into place.

Therefore, the management of the business can only be sufficient if there is a significant level of good leadership in all parameters of the startup.

The Entrepreneurial Personality

Apart from the ability to accumulate the necessary funds that would ensure good management of your business as a startup, there are specific traits required of YOU as an entrepreneur in your early years.

Harnessing these traits will translate into securing a firm position in your long term entrepreneurial journey.

These traits are general soft skills and behavioral patterns that are expected to be present in an entrepreneur whose business is still regarded as a startup.

As an entrepreneur, you must understand that sometimes the management of your business depends solely on you, not on the number of employees present.

The level of skill your least recognized staff has attained becomes irrelevant. It depends on your mindset, personality, traits, and your general perspective on your business.

Your mindset will have an effect on your startup, so embrace the entrepreneur's personality to achieve the level of success you desire for your startup.

Some of the professional leadership skills that should be present in every entrepreneur are subsequently discussed.

- **Ambition:** this refers to your ability to drive towards the achievement of a particular goal, and for this to actualize, it is required that you have specific goals and plans in place.

As the founder of a startup, it is important that you have a vision and set goals for your venture to ensure that your management is driving towards a vision, which is usually one of success.

It is required that every entrepreneur should absorb the idea of determination and hard work.

- **Tenacity:** Tenacity is the ability to persevere, to remain strong and keep moving forward no matter the situation. As a business owner who directly translates to being a leader, you will likely be found in situations that would require the exhibition of this trait, especially when you have to take risks.

  As a leader, you must be able to identify that driving factor that would assist you in providing a solution to whatever obstacle or problem that might appear as an obstruction to your business.

  Tenacity allows you to function sufficiently while you make all the needed adjustments and tweaks to your business at the beginning stages so that the growth to the success will be hitch-free.

- **Self-confidence and awareness:** in leadership, especially as an entrepreneur, the existence and recognition of "self" is highly important.

  You must be able to trust your inner voice in some situations and listen to its contributions. However, this does not mean you should be oblivious to the feelings and opinions of others on your team.

In as much as you are deeply connected with your subconscious, it is also of high importance that you are aware of those around you.

A massive part of being a leaderpernuer is found in your ability to exhibit confidence in your own judgment and also to be open to the suggestions and ideas of those in your employ.

As a leader, you must be able to exude confidence in all circumstances. Exhibit a tough inner core, speak your mind, and act decisively.

This does not mean such a leader is prideful; it merely means that you are confident in your opinions and ideas, and you trust that such a decision will not be detrimental to your business.

The existence of self-confidence and self-awareness will help keep you in check by ensuring there is no abuse of power on your part, and it eliminates any fear and instills confidence in you by your team.

- **Psychological openness:** this refers to the ability to allow the opinion of various other people. Generally, a psychologically open person is ready to adopt the principles and guidelines of others, irrespective of the differences that may exist in their lifestyle or their opinions about a particular subject.

  In this context, a leader who exhibits the trait of psychological openness is usually able to adopt the ideas of others if they are viable; he allows diverse opinions, and this supplies a broader range of knowledge from which any final decisions will be made.

In most situations, this is usually a good thing for both the leader and his business because it heightens the level of communication and productivity that exists among key employees and top management.

- **Humility:** many leaders are usually proud, and this pride is sometimes the factor that leads to their downfall.

How?

As a leaderpreneur, it is required that you continue to feed your mind with the necessary information that would keep you up to date with any of the changes and adjustments made in your industry.

Don't make the mistake of allowing yourself and your business to become vulnerable to industry changes because you stubbornly refused to stay aware of them or recognize them.

Maintain a position that requires you to learn new information and sometimes unlearn old ways in order to learn new things. In today's world, things can change quickly, and you must have an eagerness to consume all the details of change to stay on top of technology, consumer needs and views, and market trends, among other things.

As an entrepreneur, these are some of the necessary skills that are required of you, however, the management of your startup business is not restricted to these traits, there are many other features that you'll uncover through your learning and growth process.

The characteristics that have been discussed up to this point form the foundation for the rest of the process. Thus, whatever ability, trait, or personality you would like to cultivate through your journey as a leader or an entrepreneur or both have a much greater chance of success if you adopt those first steps as the foundation.

The combination of these traits and skills allow whoever possesses them to identify as a strong leader and also ensure the effective management of their business.

Professional Entrepreneurial Leadership

The personality of an entrepreneur embodies those characteristics and traits that are common in the life of most entrepreneurs, and it forms the basis of their leadership and relation with their employees and clients.

However, beyond these traits, there are some important steps and guidelines that should be employed by you as the founder and leader of a startup. These things will help ensure sound management of the business, and also to confirm your position as a good leader.

A large percentage of the world's population has identified entrepreneurship as being a dependable source of income. However, very few individuals who try their hand at entrepreneurship have the zeal, patience, and dedication to persist, nor do they devote enough of their time to developing skills and investing in themselves in a way that would influence their leadership, which, in turn, will have a direct influence on the management and productivity of their business.

This is primarily the reason why more than ninety percent of startup companies that exist in the United States end up failing.

That means only one or two succeed beyond their startup years. Most will collapse or stay stuck in this stage while the others move forward. These statistics don't bode well for you or me as an entrepreneur. Any business that is not growing, moving forward, and/or has little to no level of productivity is failing.

The failure of these startups can be attributed to various factors, such as the inability of the company to produce high-quality goods and services which consumers are always in search of. You may not be the only one with your idea. Do your research before you get started, not after you've begun to produce. Ensure that you produce a quality competitive product.

Another reason for the failure in startups is the lack of patience. Some business owners believe they have reached a level of growth where they can move to the next level (scale-up), but there's a greater risk of failure if you scale up too quickly.

For some businesses, the reason for their failure rests in ineffective leadership. They may have excellent products and services and exceptional ability to perceive the next step of growth, but their leadership skills are severely lacking. And, that will be the dynamite that destroys them.

Trust me; it's easy in business to miss something and make a critical mistake; that's why leadership is divided among departments in large corporations.

A founder of a startup who has terrible leadership skills is bound to make a critical mistake at some point, whether it's in negotiating an employee hire, losing valuable talent due to poor communication, or mismanaging contracts.

At this point, there will generally be more loss than profit as a result of poor leadership skills and the wrong attitude toward your startup. Now you think the best solution for you is to quit.

Well... it is not.

Good leadership is something learned and absorbed over years of experience. Leaders are made not born, only after they have been able to withstand a rigorous learning process. This idea is contrary to the popular opinion that leaders are born.

Of course, the circumstances of your birth and the type of socialization and nurturing you grew up with can sometimes naturally give you some leadership skills.

The truth of the matter is, you can only take natural talent so far. You must put in the work to get the correct return when it comes to leadership.

Anyone born with a flair for guiding others or tolerance for individuals or a commanding and charming personality may have people naturally drawn to them, and therefore they will have some leader identity. But there's a lot more to leadership than charm.

If you are not a born leader, it is highly possible for you to transform yourself into that level of leadership you desire and which your company--any company--needs.

Here are some guidelines for you to showcase better skills in the leadership of your startup.

1. Create plans and goals for your startup from the beginning. Often, people enter into situations and make decisions unplanned; however, this habit should never be present in your business transactions and dealings as it can be a detrimental factor moving forward.

    You must understand that your startup is yours, and you are allowed to make plans in advance for it.

    This also gives employees a clear vision of what you expect from the business and them. It defines their roles and gives them an idea of your expectations for those roles.

    Apart from this, once a plan or vision is present and you know where your startup is headed--where you want it to be--you have a blueprint for how to conduct business. A plan from the beginning would set you and the employees on the right path to effective management, and it would instill trust and belief in you and the vision for the startup.

2. **Set a good example for your employees.** Anyone who holds a position of leadership is well aware that people are watching them.

    As a leader, you have followers who look up to you. In the context of a startup, your followers are our employees, and their result and productivity are often based on how you treat them.

    A leader is not a despot, barking out orders to his subordinates.

If you want your company and its employees to behave a certain way, be that. Behave that way yourself.

- Use good listening and communication skills.
- Delegate tasks to appropriate people.
- Give and ask for feedback on projects.
- Incorporate the opinions of talented employees; give everyone a voice.
- If you're in a bind or time crunch, asking employees to stay late is something you should only do if you're willing to do it yourself.

Authentic leadership is not only about showing up with the necessary funds to control your business, but you also have to be tuned in to the feelings of your employees and lead with self-awareness.

As a leader, it is required that you lead by example. If you can do that, your employees will be ready to jump on the bandwagon of imbibing your culture without you necessarily having to make this a requirement. This cuts across all spheres, including how you dress and how well you relate with others.

Consider yourself a mentor or role model to your employees. A significant part of leading by example is communicating with your employees through your actions rather than words.

But it's also important to stay in constant communication with your employees verbally. It is also vital that you stay in communication with your employees regarding anything that may concern your startup.

Communication is the key to success in any business, and who better is there to communicate with than those individuals who are in charge of the practical work of the company, *the dirty business*.

Ensure that you mark out enough time during working hours to discuss growth with key people and anything you might have observed that requires immediate attention.

You can also communicate by entertaining the diverse opinions and ideas of the employees as it concerns the products and services of your startup.

Relating with your employees at every point should be kept positive or neutral irrespective of the topic being discussed, even if it is a loss, as you do not want to instill fear among the ranks. Fear would affect their willingness to communicate with you, and will indirectly affect the quality of products and services.

Be decisive in all situations.

Your position as a leader requires that you make the decisions that determine the direction of your startup.

Many of your decisions will be made with the *existence of doubt* and *uncertainty in your mind*, but remain transparent in the process, do the best you can with the data provided, and seek advice from others.

Ensure that even in the moments of doubt in an idea, you exude confidence in whatever decision you make because indecisiveness may cause people to lose faith and trust in you.

<u>As a leader, you need to be on top of your game, which is the reason continual learning is essential.</u>

Continued learning ensures that your knowledge is updated to the newest cutting edge innovations in your industry. That way, no idea will ever appear foreign or new to you. And don't forget to keep up with the progress and market status of your competitors!

Learn from your mistakes.

In an entrepreneur's journey as in life, especially as a leader, mistakes are inevitable. However, these mistakes can be a significant learning ground for you.

You must understand that not every decision will work for you but what significantly differentiates a good leader from any other Tom, Dick, and Harry running a business is their ability to grow and move beyond that mistake and gain valuable lessons from it.

Every failure should be viewed as a success--as having learned what does and/or does not work.

It is essential that you do not dwell on mistakes; however, it is also required that you acknowledge them before you move forward. This way, you won't repeat them. If you can do this, then you have set a useful example for your employees, and they will also follow suit.

As a brief sidenote, let me talk about employee loyalty and your vision. As your internal culture starts to develop among employees, you'll begin to see three different types: drillers, passengers, and rowers.

Drillers are toxic individuals. At every opportunity, they will talk down the company. The rule is to find them fast and weed them out. This may sound harsh, but it's either them or you and the many good workers who rely on the company for their livelihoods. These folks can ruin your company before your company gets its footing in the market.

Passengers take no initiative; they're happy to vocalize all that is wrong but do nothing themselves to fix problems or offer solutions. Give yourself and them ninety days to convert their attitude and work ethic. If they can't change, excise them.

Rowers are the best employees. They behave more like owners than workers. They rarely complain, and if they do, you should listen to them. They get on with it and go the extra mile, always looking for ways to improve the company with ideas and potential solutions to problems.

Take responsibility when things go wrong and show humility. Humility is one of the traits associated with leadership when there is a victory or success in your business. People will heap praises on you. However, you must not allow this to control you--in other words, don't let it go to your head.

Instead of channeling the adoration and compliments to the path of pride, direct it in a way that will enable you to achieve more success. And don't forget to give credit to employees who made the success possible.

Likewise, when things go wrong in the startup, irrespective of whoever caused it, people are always going to blame you.

It is your startup; therefore, tale responsibility for shortcomings and do not attempt to blame others. This will only cause low morale among the ranks. Your employees will view you as a great and humble leader and will award you their respect.

Being a great leader is highly essential in whatever you do in business. Your company's growth is almost always a direct reflection of you and you're ability to make decisions.

5

Chapter Five: Advancement Via Leadership

Various businesses exist across the world and in every community; they usually have different goals. However, there is one thing every business has in common: their need to grow, to move beyond the initial position of the company when it was just a startup. This is what is referred to as the advancement of the company.

Every company employs distinctive strategies to ensure that their company is in a definite position for growth.

However, some specific guidelines can be adopted through the journey to advancement.

It is undoubtedly your desire to move forward, to grow and progress in size, earnings, and market recognition.

However, most entrepreneurs find this difficult to achieve, not because they are not equipped with resources, but because of their ignorance regarding strategic positioning. It is for this reason that I have deemed it essential to discuss some of the skills and ideas that would ensure the growth of your business beyond a typical startup.

The success of a startup is determined by the relationship that exists between both the employees and the employer as well as their ability to dedicate their skills collectively to the full development of the business.

Therefore, as a leader, you must be able to secure a stable relationship between yourself and your employees, as well as ensure that a cordial relationship exists amongst your team.

This is referred to as organization culture--the interplay among employees--and goes back to the individual types of people you have working for you. If there's a bad seed among employees, it will directly affect everyone's performance and therefore the success of your business.

Everyone needs to be able to work together effectively as a team. Therefore, as a leader, you must be willing to monitor the relationship, production, and productivity of the group, and also be able to exhibit a fraction of self-awareness.

Your ability as a leader requires that you are able to secure the following techniques in creating and retaining a secure relationship between your employees and with you.

- **Define your vision and goals.** Apart from defining your goals and having a clear vision for it in your mind, you must be able to communicate that vision to your team.
  Leading an entrepreneurial journey, especially a startup, is not a one-person show. You must communicate your vision, goals, and aspiration to every employee, so they are not functioning at different ends.

  Begin with a meeting of all employees to clarify their roles and what's expected of them. This would also be done at the initial interview stage, but it's best to avoid confusion, frustration, and competition among employees by reiterating each person's role and duties.

Allow everyone to have a voice and be open to questions. Suggestions should be noted and looked at in your private time. You can then get back to employees regarding any new decisions.

The relationship among people that exists in every business is highly important because a troubled employee might just be the starting point for the collapse of the entire company.

If the employees do not feel comfortable or confident in the workplace, they begin to leave, and your level of productivity faces a downfall. This type of relationship should not be your only concern; you should also be self-aware of the level of connection that exists between you, the employer, and these employees.

Some of the guidelines that help to sustain a good relationship with your employees have been discussed in previous chapters; however, this section is dedicated to highlighting some of the things that must be avoided if you aim to strengthen your relationship.

In many startup companies and developing companies, new employees usually depend on veteran employees. However, when these "mentors" in a particular workplace begin to leave increasingly, it plants a seed of doubt in the minds of other employees, and they, in turn, may begin to look for other possible employers.

It does not even matter if they do not have a substantial reason to leave on their own, but the perception that something is amiss and causing top employees to leave is enough to convince them that there is something wrong with the startup.

How then does an increase in individuals resigning affect your business?

The more people you lose, the more your productivity drops. Therefore, to secure advancement, ensure that you are able to retain your employees by eliminating fear and doubt in your vision and goal.

To sustain your advancement, you must respect an employee's decision to resign, but always try to get to the reason they're leaving. It may not be as a result of any of the factors discussed above.

If you feel they are valuable to you, discuss ways to make them happy in their position. Your goal is to retain a valuable employee, not to give them whatever they want. You want loyalty, not blackmail.

It is essential you understand that employee turnover will be part of your company's journey. Employees come and go, and an employee may decide to resign even after various attempts by you to allow him to retain his position. You can't hold someone forcefully unless they're under contract, and to do so can affect the general level of productivity of your business.

- **Seek mentorship and networking.** In the world of entrepreneurship, mentorship is essential, and although this is generally expected to be beneficial, it sometimes becomes the opposite. It becomes counterproductive when you are more concerned with the idea of a mentor rather than the ideas and direction he or she might be offering or the vision you have for your company.

One of the most effective mentor-mentee relationships that exist might mean that the mentor is unaware of his position. The reality is mentors are everywhere, and information is very common now. Therefore, you should be concerned with the knowledge that could assist you in understanding more than regular commonplace things.

Also, be sure to network if you find the opportunity. If you have the opportunity to be around someone you admire, attempt to make a connection and relate outside work. This makes mentorship easier and more adaptable for you.

- **Define what you would like to build from your startup.** In some cases, having an idea at the beginning of your business may not be enough to secure its advancement. If your growth expectations are based on the percentage of productivity rises, you will need to clarify the products and services that your business will provide in its future.

Once you've defined this, you will find it easy to adopt the necessary resources and opportunities at your disposal. If you can highlight the services and products you would like to present to consumers at every level of advancement, you will have clear goals by which to measure your success.

Be flexible.

Adjust your products and services to fit the consumer's stage and position, but don't radically change your business model if it fits your vision. For example, Apple has changed its products several times, from computers to phones to music devices to watches. Each business segment can stand on its own but together it forms the Apple Ecosystem.

The introduction of Tim Cook's leadership led to the continued vision laid out originally by Steve Jobs. Apple's vision statement is bold yet vague regarding how the business is run, while its Mission Statement dives deeper into the collaboration of the various business segments.

Apple's Vision Statement:
We believe that we are on the face of the earth to make great products and that's not changing. We are constantly focusing on innovating. We believe in the simple not the complex.

We believe that we need to own and control the primary technologies behind the products that we make, and participate only in markets where we can make a significant contribution. We believe in saying no to thousands of projects, so that we can really focus on the few that are truly important and meaningful to us.

We believe in deep collaboration and cross-pollination of our groups, which allow us to innovate in a way that others cannot. And frankly, we don't settle for anything less than excellence in every group in the company, and we have the self-honesty to admit when we're wrong and the courage to change.

And I think regardless of who is in what job those values are so embedded in this company that Apple will do extremely well.

No matter how many product lines or software Apple launches, one thing has not changed. They have been able to remain within a particular field of productivity, a field that continually answers their primary reason, which is to make the life of their consumers better through technological innovations.

The longterm success, advancement, and sustainability of any business is mostly dependent on its leader's ability to maximize resources and opportunities duly.

Ensure that you have carried out adequate research in your area of specialty. Having identified the business idea that best sits well with you, it is required that you move towards identifying the potential benefits and the resources that are necessary for such a business. This would, in turn, assist you in setting certain expectations for your business.

Communicate performance standards in the workplace clearly for every employee.

Chapter Six: Effective Pipeline Management

Pipeline management is a technique of Customer Relationship Management (CRM). It is an extension of CRM focused on ensuring that you have a standard ongoing relationship and is also a tool dedicated to ensuring that you have set plans to oversee and direct your sales goals (a.k.a "the sales pipeline").

Pipeline management is a tool and process commonly used by the sales team of a startup in determining the past and present sales statistics and future sales projections of a company.

Sales pipeline management lays the foundation for nearly every sale a startup has and is essential to help project future revenue. The success and development of a company are mostly dependent on the percentage of sales such a company can make.

Although pipeline management assists in identifying your position and expectations with your consumers, it also assists the business in increasing revenue projections as it helps the sales team to remain focused and organized with where each customer is on the purchasing journey.

Pipeline Management Strategies

As a leaderpreneur or any individual in the entrepreneurial sector, you should already be aware that the apex of the business relies on your level of sales and your company's relation to its consumers. The only way to understand what's happening with this is through effective pipeline management.

However, the problem with many startups is not that they are ignorant of the importance of effective pipeline management, but that they are unable to execute specific guidelines and practices.

This was sufficiently proven in a study by Vantage Point and the Sales Management Association, which discovered that 61% of sales managers claimed not to have received any training on pipeline management.

In comparison, 63% also claimed that their company's pipeline management is terrible.

The number of people who truly understand the effectiveness of pipeline management is limited, and it would benefit you, especially if you are the Chief Executive Officer or founder, to understand this strategy for advancing your startup.

It is for this reason that I have deemed it important to provide some of the practices that would undoubtedly provide you with effective pipeline management.

The procedure of pipeline management may appear cumbersome to some extent. However, the adoption of a step-by-step technique will immediately assist you in your planning because pipeline management goes beyond marketing; it also involves resource management, financial planning, and sales maturity.

- The first step is to identify and develop your *pipeline stages*. The pipeline stages refer to the visualization of stages that would lead to the eventual sales of your goods and services. There are no definitive requirements of the pipeline because they differ based on the specificities of each business, however, there are five stages that are commonly found in general guidelines.

Setting up these stages in your pipeline creates a level of ease in your funnel-tracking software, and allows the sales team to discern information from a single glance, such as the sales team's progress, options to create reasonable sales goals and forecast potential profit, and the number of leads available at each stage. This puts everything that concerns sales in order.

However, before we proceed to the other steps of pipeline management, I must emphasize the importance of the goal, which is to keep the leads interested through certain activities until they make the decision to purchase.

Stage 1: The initial contact stage or "prospecting".

This is when fresh leads contact your startup or you reach out to them.

At this point, they are nothing other than just leads or points of contact to the business. The possibility that they will turn into paying clients is hardly discernable in this stage.

However, you must continue to present excellent communication and begin to establish a relationship with this potential customer.

Input all leads into your CRM so you can monitor them. The choice to manually input contacts or automatically upload your leads with a tool is entirely left to you.

After the step of uploading these contacts into your CRM, then the room for contact is officially open, this is done via cold emails and cold calls to determine which of the leads are interested in the goods and services you are willing to offer.

There are various methods of establishing an email campaign to keep potential buyers informed of what you are doing and what you have to offer. Be sure to look into the various methods and features your CRM provides.

Stage 2: Decide if the leads are qualified.

After the series of cold calls and/or cold emails, it is highly possible that most of the leads contacted are interested in your services.

Although many of them have shown interest, this does not mean that they are all willing to purchase your goods or services. Therefore, at this point, you are left to define the leads that are most likely to make purchases and prioritize these leads.

(In some startups, such as those who provide SaaS or Mobile apps, this phase may be partially automated. Inbound traffic to a landing page or downloading the app may instantly qualify a lead. However, churn in these types of businesses is real and will need to be addressed in a similar fashion to keep user retention high.)

Leads that show further interest by asking to speak to the salesperson or asking further questions about the services provided are regarded as Sales-Qualified Leads (SQLs).

Stage 3: The meeting.

Once an ordinary lead moves to this stage, it belongs to the SQLs and has to show undoubted interest by making a further inquiry about the goods and services provided.

It is at this stage that it is best to consider a one-on-one meeting with such individuals; this could be a live demo or an online call between you and the client.

(Again, offering a SaaS and/or mobile may mean this stage is related to inbound inquiries such as webpage chatbot interactions, email correspondence, or phone calls. Many lower cost items may not require as many sales steps as more expensive or complicated products.)

However, it is essential that whatever presentation is made to these people is tailored in a way that would highlight how your services are targeted towards achieving their desires or creating a solution they desire.

Stage 4: The proposal.

At this point, it is expected that you should have offered the lead a proposal or you are still within the process of drawing up one. Thus, this stage means that the leads are considering whether to purchase your products or not.

Stage 5: The closing.

From the beginning, the aim of this is to gain a purchase; it is at this point you can adequately discern if you have been able to properly execute the requirements of each of the other stages based on the feedback of the lead.

However, the closing may not be as smooth as expected; sometimes the pipeline management stages end at the proposal, as the eventual closing--the sale--is dependent on the ability of the team to follow through. Getting this lead as a customer is dependent on your ability to consistently follow-up until the lead signs the proposal.

- **Learn how to identify quality streams.**

    The entire success of pipeline management is dependent on leads, and not only the quantity of leads that you are able to bring into the company, but also the quality.

    Therefore, having set up your pipeline management technique, improve your method of contacting leads and ensure you are able to establish a consistent model of introducing new potentials and priorities to the pipeline.

    Finding leads is key to the success of your business because the more you have, the higher the possibility of developing and growing your startup.

- **Learn to categorize and prioritize.**

    In as much as the success of your business is dependent on leads, you may not be able to accept all the willing leads. In most situations, quality is more important than quantity. Therefore, as some leads become customers and new prospects are inputted, it is essential that you categorize and determine which are worth more of your time.

    This technique will assist you in identifying those leads with higher possibilities of patronage and will allow you to devote more attention to those leads, which would undoubtedly remain under your belt till the closing stage. Thus, you are required to create a board that would assist your sales team and personnel to quickly identify those SQLs and other leads which have exhibited the greatest interest.

- **Cleanup your pipeline regularly.** If you are the kind of entrepreneur who is reluctant to let go of leads even after they have stopped showing interest in your business, then you will eventually find yourself with a clustered pipeline.

    Apart from clustering the pipeline, it also has an adverse effect on the forecasting of sales by skewing the numbers, and it deprives you of clearly identifying other transactions that would have been successful. It is vital that you understand that if a lead has remained on your pipeline for an extended period without purchasing, this is a clear pointer that it will not close anytime soon. Their duration on the pipeline determines the eventual success of leads.

    Although it might be difficult to abandon some of the leads, especially when you have become extremely attached to them, it is required that you clean up regularly to allow the new opportunities a chance to succeed.

The sales pipeline management technique can assist you in ensuring that you gain more value and profit from your sales opportunities.

Without this knowledge, most businesses will remain unaware of the detriment they are causing to the growth of their business due to their ignorance of sales patterns.

Pointers To Change Your Pipeline Management

Pipeline management is one of the crucial components to any business, however, you may have the knowledge of the existence of a pipeline but do not possess the skills and techniques for its effective implementation.

Many times when businesses experience some degree of loss in their progress, they immediately search for adjustments that can be made to their sales process. It's quickly concluded that an increase in sales generation is needed. Although this might be a possible solution, it is rarely the singular solution.

For you to understand the cause of the decline that has occurred in your business, it is essential that you look at every sector of your sales--the entire sales process, not only one section.

The sales process is referred to as the sales pipeline, and it is on this that the success of the whole business is dependent. However, there could be other things that may be wrong with your business.

If you find any of the following factors present in your business, then maybe an evaluation or change of pipeline management is in order.

- **Generality in the treatment of customers.** You treat every customer the same way and do not react based on the foundation and values of customers individually.

Therefore, you must identify the peculiarities of each customer. In your interaction with customers, each group or individual wants to feel like they are getting their own unique experience.

Every human generally wants to feel special. Apart from this technique assisting you in sustaining a customer, it also helps the customer to feel more comfortable with you, building brand loyalty and extending the life of the relationship.

- **A clustered pipeline.** If you are an individual who hardly ever declutters the pipeline--prioritizes leads based on those willing to close a deal with you and those who are not--this is an obvious pointer that something in your pipeline management requires a change.

Possibly, many of the sales that you thought would reach the closing stage in no time have taken more time than expected, and only a few are closing deals with you. If this is your situation, you must realize that more important than getting leads is closing deals with the leads you have.

Leads are of no use to the business if they cannot be converted to actual sales. Therefore, as the leaderpreneur, it is expected that you motivate your sales personnel to be more effective in their procedures and ensure these leads are converted to actual sales.

What use is a handful of leads if they cannot provide you with real profits?

- **The duration to close a deal is extended.** If you as the leader of a startup feel like the time it takes for a special deal to be actualized is too long, imagine how the customer might feel. Although you do not want to coerce a customer into a contract with you, you also do not want to allow them too much time to overthink purchasing your goods or services.

    In some cases, the customer needs a little push. You could offer that assistance to them by asking appropriate questions that will identify their reluctance to close the deal. This does not imply that you become a pest or nuisance to your customers.

    You simply want to find out the source of their resistance. Most of the time, it's emotional. People buy for emotional reasons. They want a product or service to make them feel good about themselves and their lives.

    Just a few reminders would do the trick. Explain your solution in such a way that your potential customer can envision themselves using this product or service.

    Have a few email reminders set up to remind them of the benefits of your goods and services. Use testimonials from other satisfied customers.

Always answer the "Why buy?" and be sure to find how YOUR way, YOUR product, and/or YOUR service makes life easier for the customer.

If there is one sales takeaway you will want to tweet from this book, here it is:
DO NOT TRY TO SELL BASED ON FEATURES OR FUNCTION.

Sales are made when an emotional connection is made--where the customer understands that a
level of comfort will be provided when they become YOUR client.

- **You feel like you are spending too much time on administration.** If this is how you are feeling, then this is your truth.

So, you are spending more than a reasonable amount of time on the administration of the startup, rather than generating sales and increasing the conversion rates?

Although, it might seem challenging, layout a simple plan for generating sales and conversion that would help the problem and follow through with the plan by scheduling in enough time to deal with it.

- **You do not follow up on your customers after sales are made.** Follow-up is essential in creating a good relationship with customers; beyond the purchase of goods and services, it is necessary to ensure proper contact with the customer to assess their satisfaction.

It is through continual communication that you can determine if a client is satisfied with your services or not, and it is through follow-up that you can receive reviews and make adjustments suggested by a customer.

If you do not follow up and the client finds something wrong in the product, if this kind of person chooses to avoid contacting you, then you have created a loss for your business. You've also lost the opportunity to get feedback that might improve your awareness of how customers use your products.

Thus, if the customer presents complaints, ensure that you handle it immediately, and if you have another product that could serve as an alternative to the initial purchase, give it to them. This way, you have developed your relationship with your clients further, and this creates the idea that you not only care about the money, but you also care about the customer's satisfaction.

- **You are unable to show and tell.** If you happen to be marketing your services over the phone or trying to pitch a product to an investor, it is essential that you are able to talk about your company and it's services and goals in 30-60 seconds.

In an online presentation, about page or sales page, this would amount to no more than one page or about 300 easily scannable words. You should not only be willing to tell your client about what you do, but you should find a way to show them the goods.

Beyond sales pipeline management, some other factors must be considered in the accountability of a business:

Customer validation. This is an aspect of the customer development exercise which assists you in determining whether your assumptions about your customers are correct. It is used to determine if the information gathered in customer discovery is accurate and defines how this information and details can be implemented into your general business plan or model.

It is not enough to assume that customers would purchase some specific products based on their demographic or use history. Individuals are allowed to change their minds and opinions of things. Therefore, this validation proves the relevance and authenticity of your research before you start to spend money on the project.

Operational and functional qualification. Operation qualification is targeted towards ensuring that the business, while still in its pre-manufacturing or pre-money stage, is able to exhibit the potential for achieving its operational goals and requirements.

At the level of determining operational qualification, the startup is tested for its ability to create the expected solution, prove the Minimal Viable Product, or achieve its set goals.

Functional qualification, on the other hand, is aimed towards taking test runs concerning the functions and requirements of business before its effectiveness is decided.

As presented through this chapter, pipeline management begins from the moment of initial contact with a lead.

Still, it does not end till well after the time of purchase, and sometimes the entire process exists beyond that, which is follow-up with the goal of maintaining a loyal following to your brand.

Therefore, in your sales of goods, tech, and/or services your aim should be towards the conclusion that your customers be as comfortable and confident with the products as you are.

Chapter Seven: Administration & Leadership

The systems of administration and leadership are two principles that work in close collaboration.

Although these principles are different when you consider their general meaning, in the context of business, the success of one usually ensures the success of the other, which clearly demonstrates their individual importance.

The administration of a startup is dependent on the kind of leadership put in place, and the leadership structure of any business is dependent on the administration format.

These principles should be established during the founding of every startup as is they are a major determinant of the eventual success and growth or failure and stagnation of a company.

The principles are initially determined by the traits and relationships that exist between the employer and the employees.

Through the course of this chapter, I'll give you some of the important strategies in choosing the right employees for your business and the best techniques for sustaining a good relationship between employer and employee.

Choosing Your Employees

At an early stage, many businesses make the mistake of hiring just about anybody who comes to them during their recruitment because they feel the need to get started.

They tend to hurry this important phase and settle for whatever comes their way. However, this should not be the case even if you are in desperate need of help.

Your recruitment efforts should be based on your objectives, goals, and vision for the company, thereby ensuring that you employ individuals who are most able to assist you in achieving these objectives.

An entrepreneur can birth the idea of a business, but the core of the business is in the hands of the business representatives--YOUR employees.

Therefore, you must be critical and evaluative in your recruitment process so that you only employ people who would help to achieve your entrepreneurial dream in the best way possible.

They must be completely on board with your vision and be able to express that back to you so you're sure they understand what's expected of them.

The following are some strategies that are directed towards improving your recruitment process, so that you do not dismiss the right candidates and employ the ones who are wrong for your business.

- **Identify their competence.** Use whatever technique is available to you to screen potential employees; it is important that you are able to identify their level of competence for your business.

    This is a major factor to be considered, and it entails questioning their correctness for a particular position, whether they have the right skills, education, and experience to fit within the parameters of your business.

    Once the initial background and experiencee check is completed, have each potential candidate come in for a one-on-one interview with you and probe their intentions as well as their expectations. Often, accepting a position is less about the salary than about being able to achieve something within the company. This is particularly true of creatives and technical people.

- **Are they capable?** Many times during the process of recruitment, many entrepreneurs are faced with candidates who have the perfect skills and qualifications for their business. A more important question exists in their ability to flourish in a particular business environment, especially if they have little to no experience in such an area.

Capability can be described differently by various entrepreneurs, but a specific factor can be generalized. When faced with the idea of describing capability, most answers are always in tune with whether a particular client is adaptable and willing to grow and take more responsibilities through the years.

It is important to highlight whether a particular candidate is able to adapt to any and every position during the recruitment process. Are they suited to only one aspect? If this is a highly technical area of expertise, it may be okay to leave them in one position.

- **Are they compatible?** Will they fit into the existing employee culture? Personalities can clash. If you found a qualified candidate, but you feel this person is going to be a prima donna, don't hire them.

A potential employee may constantly have to communicate; communicate with their employer, consumers, and even other employees. The success of your business is, to some extent, dependent on the relationship that exists between employees and with those employees who will act as the company's representatives with customers.

Therefore, ensure that you find someone who works well with

others; who is compatible with others. Ensure that the person has a harmonious and willing character.

- **Question their commitment.** As a business that is in its early stages, you should avoid the constant turnover of employees. Every time you hire someone, they need to be trained and evaluated. If there is a constant turnover, this wastes valuable time and resources on your part.

  Factors that could lead to this are incompetent employees, personality clashes, and employee's early retirement; both can be avoided if an entrepreneur is extremely critical before employment. Don't be sentimental about this. it's either them or your company. Within the recruitment stage, ensure that you find out a potential hire's level of seriousness and dedication to your business.

  The less turnover you have, the less it will affect the company's administration and productivity.

  A critical evaluation of their past jobs can give you an insight into the person's level of commitment. Look for trends in behavior, such as quitting in a few months, being written up for bad behavior, and so on.

- **Define the person's character.** One factor most entrepreneurs rarely consider is the character of the candidate. Ensure that their character and values align with yours and the company's to avoid conflict that limits productivity and growth on the part of the employee.

  You see, no company attains and retains success on its own. You might have the capital, the vision, and the goals to start a business, but the eventual success is determined by your ability to employ the right people.

  If you are able to adhere to some of the strategies presented, I am certain that you will be able to build a successful enterprise in your area of specialization.

Leading Your Employees

The success of your company as it concerns administration and leadership is not solely dependent on just a particular group of people. The administration aspect may depend on your employees, but the bulk of leadership work is on you.

As the leader of a startup, the leaderpreneur, there are expectations that go beyond your objectives and visions for the business.

This particular strategy that is going to be discussed is a major factor in leading your employees towards achieving your set goals for the business.

Beyond selecting the right candidates during the recruitment process, you must be equipped with certain properties to guide your leadership. As much as it is important that you employ people who are willing and ready to submit to your authority, be cooperative, and get their expected jobs done, you, as the leader of the startup, must be able to provoke that obligation to follow your guidance without stating it explicitly or forcing this situation.

Therefore, to achieve the maximum capacity of efficiency in your employees, some techniques that can be adopted by you as their leader are discussed in subsequent paragraphs.

Create the right environment and culture. The first step to effective leadership is to create an environment that allows it to thrive. Firstly, I would like you to imagine the different ranks that exist in the military and wonder how they are able to provoke such a level of selflessness and respect among themselves and for their leaders.

The answer to this is found in the kind of environment that's fostered among all ranks. For military personnel, it is such that they are not given a choice to deter from the culture that's been honed over many years of leadership skills and experience. The environment has created the culture, and they have imbibed this reality.

However, this type of loyalty is not limited to only the workings of the military. Your ability to lead your employees properly is dependent on the culture and qualities that you have presented to them from the start of their employment.

Delegate wisely. The next thing to do in the management of your employees through your position as a leader is to delegate wisely. The main reason people are employed in the first place is to delegate authority and activities. However, it is not enough to just delegate. You must do it wisely.

Delegate responsibility among employees based n their ability to get things done, their experiencee in supervising, and their basic nature; can they do this effectively without creating a bad feeling among those they're supervising?

Many leaderpreneurs believe they should be in control of whatever activities they have delegated. They try to micro-manage everyone and everything. This can be a huge disaster. Not only would it be extremely exhausting to do this, but in doing so, you demoralize employees by not showing them you trust them enough to work independently and get the job done.

You may not have the stamina, flexibility, and skill to supervise every aspect of your company to the point that it would provide outstanding results.

When you delegate, you have increased the percentage of tasks that can be completed, as well as ensured that you have qualitative results.

Monitor employee progression. Not micro-managing doesn't mean you should have blinders on when it comes to task completion. Your job is to keep an eye on those employees to whom you've delegated responsibility, not in standing over their shoulders watching everything they do, but in checking in to be sure they and their team are progressing within the time frame designated for particular tasks.

Set employee goals. At this point, you are certainly aware that goals are an important part of every business; it guides production, management, and success. However, beyond setting general goals for the business, you can also set goals for your employees at the start of each working year. This drives and expands their productivity.

Apart from them achieving these individual goals, it drives them towards achieving the overall vision that you have for the company. Therefore, set explicit and concise goals for each employee or department and monitor their progress towards this goal.

Encourage open communication. This is key in every relationship that exists between humans, even in business.

Far too many leaderpreneurs believe they should keep to themselves, looming around their business environment with the idea, "It is my business, I can run it; however, I like."

You should understand that although it is your business it is essential that you have constant communication with employees; keep them updated concerning the latest news about your business and ask for their opinions and ideas that they think should be added or subtracted regarding their own role in the business.

If you consider it, a huge increase in profit might be possible because the employees are the ones in the field, the ones who usually take a critical examination of the business.

More than most entrepreneurs might like to admit, your employees usually have and know the best business ideas. Apart from this, it also makes it easier for you to identify if employees have not been efficient in their roles.

Celebrate your employee's achievements and growth. In as much as you may feel entitled to whatever progress they have brought to your company because you pay them, it's alwayss a good idea to share the credit.

To establish a good and long-standing relationship, you should cultivate the habit of appreciation and recognition. This creates and sustains good employer-employee relationships.

Many employees crave the recognition of their bosses, and when celebrated, it encourages them to do better and other employees to increase their productivity level. You do not have to make a grand gesture to show your appreciation, but mentioning that you have noticed someone's hard work or success is a good start.

For major company successes or milestones, show you're appreciation on a grander scale; maybe a company picnic or a half day on Friday or a bonus if you can afford these things.

Managing Your Employees

With the information that has been provided in this book, it should not be news to you when I say the management of employees can either make or break your business.

However, employee management is not nearly as simple as you might think, especially when you are leading a big and successful company, which more often than not directly means that you have different kinds of people working for you; people with different backgrounds, cultures, belief systems, motivations, goals, and work ethics.

You should not let this bother you because, with careful and skillful employee management techniques, you can capitalize on their strengths and use them to achieve the team's general vision.

The following are some employee management techniques that will ensure that you, as a leader, create a work environment that enables your employees to perform at their best capacity, thereby achieving maximum productivity in your business.

At the beginning of your business, that is, in its early years or as a startup, you should create an employee management system that allows you to monitor your employees properly and effectively. In creating an effective performance management system, some components are standard requirements that should be in place.

- **Create clear job descriptions.** Before you hire someone, give them a complete job description of what you need them to do--what's expected of them--so they have all the information they need to make the decision to accept the position. The more a potential employee knows up front, the more likely they are to be an asset to the company.

  Upon employing someone, reiterate clearly the defined role, position, and expectations of that individual so he can actively function in such a position.

  Apart from functioning actively, it also helps to avoid personality clashes and arguments in the workplace. For instance, you have employed two people to stay at your front office, but you had two entirely different roles for them but failed to state these roles explicitly. There could be a clash in heirarchy or even worse, inefficiency.

  People tend to be ineffective in activities where they are not the only one delegated to it. Therefore, ensure that you clearly state the role of each employee and the expectations you have for each of them. This makes effectiveness and accountability easy.

- **Negotiate the terms of employment immediately after recruitment.** Conflict is not only between employees. Some employees will have issues or conflicts with their employer at different employment stages for different reasons.

  However, the one reason being considered here is the lack of clarity in the employment contract. Some businesses do not even have a contract, which can be harmful to your business. Before you employ anyone irrespective of your relationship with such a person, ensure that they understand and agree to the terms of the employment being offered. This is important because they might request to leave halfway through their service to your company, and this type of turnover is highly detrimental to the growth of your business. You may have invested money in training; employees may be privy to proprietary information; a key employee who wants to leave may leave an unacceptable gap in productivity, leaving remaining employees to do their work and potentially affecting the relationship that exists between employees. Not having a pre-employment contract in place exhibits lack of foresight and planning, and shows weakness in your leadership.

- **Discuss employees' expectations and standards.** The role of discussion or communication in a business cannot be overemphasized.

  It is essential that you take time to discuss what you expect from every employee or department. Talk to employees and department heads individually at every stage of your business growth. A huge percentage of your company's success is embedded in discussion and communication about progress, standards, and shortfalls. Keep employees updated about plan changes, innovations, and new expectations to move everyone forward and expand from a particular point of the business.

- **Provide career and skill development opportunities.** Most people who resign from a particular business leave because they feel the company no longer offers them the opportunity for growth. So they begin the search for a new job opportunity.

  It's generally difficult to keep this a secret when it occurs, which gives you, the owner, the opportunity have a discussion with an employee who is unhappy with their position, for whatever reason. If the employee is worth keeping, give them more responsibility or a more prestigious position, If possible.

To avoid this altogether, you can offer career upgrades and business masterclasses to ensure that your employees enjoy continual knowledge upgrades and are not limited by you. If your employees show interest in learning outside the company, then you must allow them to reach out to learn from resources and people outside the company.

- **Create a culture of mentorship.** It is in your best interest as a leaderpreneur to create an environment that encourages mentorship. This allows employees to be accountable to someone outside their focus areas, and such a person usually provides encouragement, which continually fuels their effectiveness.

Evaluation of Assets and Liabilities

Every entrepreneur should understand the financial position of his or her business, as this is a major factor in determining its total value.

However, the case is such that very few individuals understand the process and requirements of valuing one's business. Although it might initially look like a load of work, it is hardly as difficult as people make it seem.

In the assessment of your business, two specific factors are considered and calculated to determine the final position of your business: *assets* and *liabilities*.

Assets generally are things that can be said to hold value, something most individuals are familiar with. For instance, the valuable diamond necklace that you received from your grandmother can be regarded as an asset. However, in a business, company assets should alwayss appear on the balance sheet and may consist of land, buildings, equipment, available cash, and stocks--anything that increases the general worth of a company.

However, assets are not only tangible; they could also include intangibles such as a will or access to credit. Therefore, the type of assets every company has varies based on the size and percentage of materials such a company is able to acquire.

Assets fall into two categories: *fixed* and *current* assets. Current assets include cash and any other thing that can be converted to cash within the year it was acquired. Fixed assets are things like land, buildings, and the overall value of your brand or the percentage of it you own.

Liabilities are the direct opposite of assets. Assets would make you richer to some extent, but liabilities are debts; they are any debts owed by you or the company. This debt includes a mortgage, bank loans, commitment to investors, and leases on equipment, among other things.

Exactly like assets, there are two major types of liabilities: current liabilities and non-current liabilities. The current ones are the debts that demand payment within the next few months or year, while the latter refers to debts that are owed beyond the next twelve months. That is any debt that is owed beyond a year.

Apart from your position as a leader and your employees determining the success of your business, the level of assets and the range of liabilities owed by a company can either make or break a company, depending on your production.

Chapter Eight: Relationship Building

"Even the Lone Ranger didn't do it alone."
~Harvey Mackay

Reread the opening statement. That covers everything this chapter is about. It is crucial for you as a business leader to pay attention to relationship building. It is common knowledge that teamwork tends to thrive better as "two heads are better than one."

As the leader of a business, don't be so focused on the product or service you're offering that you shove business relationships to the side. It is not enough to have that winning business idea or concept; seeing it materialize is just as important, and for that to happen, other people have to be involved.

The smooth sailing of your business isn't yours to ensure alone, but that of everyone involved in your business. This brings us to the importance of good business relationships.

Just like real-life relationships, business relationships require effort and intentionality too. As a leader, you have to be ready to build a good open business relationship with employees, managers, clients, vendors, investors, bankers, and anyone else you deal with if you want your business to thrive. Every process involved in that finished product or service is essential, and the people guiding those processes are equally as relevant, if not more important.

In the previous chapter, I walked you through the process of requirement and the relevance of that process.

It is not enough to recruit the best in every field; you must maintain a good relationship with each of these recruits so that everyone brings their A-game every day. Your relationship with each teammate is what forms the foundation of teamwork.

Let me walk you through the process of watering the plants of business relationships.

Intentionality

What does it mean to be intentional? Simply put, it means that an action is premeditated and purposeful; it's done in a deliberate manner to achieve an intended result. This is always the first step for me.

Being intentional about the kind of relationships you want to build in your business sets the pace for the actions that follow. Despite it requiring work on your part, you are dealing with real humans and everything that comes with that fact: emotions, feelings, personalities, moods, experiences, history, self-esteem, individual perception, and so on.

So being intentional helps you realize the extent you want to go with these relationships and when or where you would want to draw the line.

Intentionality is the quality that will guide your actions towards building a healthy work relationship. It will help you control your words and actions. If you are intentional about making your business space a safe place for your workers, then that will lead you always to make sure your workers can express themselves as well as share life problems that can affect their productivity at work.

If your goal is to ensure mutual respect, you will always be guided to accord them respect in your words and actions even when they are out of place. This is what will form the basis of your relationship with your staff. The results you want to achieve--your goal for the relationship--will be informed by your predetermined intention.

So, when you have a goal or desire towards your relationship with your workers, it is necessary to be intentional about those goals or aspirations and let this intention serve as a controlling force for both your words and actions.

Communication

Communication is a vital component in building any kind of relationship, and business relationships are not excluded. For there to be a relationship in the first place, there has to be effective communication.

Effective communication opens the ground for a relationship, and it has so much positive impact in ensuring not just a business relationship but a *healthy* business relationship.

As the leader and business head, you have to create open and honest communication among your employees. You have to learn to speak to them and listen to them too. This instills confidence and trust in you. It also prevents discord among workers and helps to prevent employee turnover.

Do not mistake one-sided speaking as communication; to ensure effective communication, you have to make sure your employees are allowed to speak freely, thereby making them more willing and inclined to listen to you--to hear and absorb what you're saying. Allow them to air their opinions on business ideas, concepts, processes and methods, goods, and services.

Ensure you are confident enough to accept constructive criticisms as their views may not always be in your favor.

Create comprehensive strategies to communicate with your workers, which might include creating some kind of work activity where you and your employees sit together to review business decisions and matters and make it a safe period where your employees can air their honest opinions.

It could also be making time to communicate one on one with each of your employees. This way, employees who are shy or introverted and cannot speak up in public spaces can have a chance to air their views.

If you do not have enough time to communicate with your employees actively, you can assign that task to a high standing employee like the manager or HR personnel who would do this on your behalf and give you feedback on whatever the employees say. That way, less time is required from you, and you can respond to their questions or thoughts.

Only delegate communication tasks if you do not have enough time to properly dedicate yourself to the task personally.

No one can do it like you or give you more accurate feedback than when you do it yourself.

Effective communication makes your employees feel like their opinions are valued, and this would work as a positive driving force for them to do their best at their different tasks. It also reduces the chance of work misunderstandings and problems.

Giving your employees an active voice in the running of the company provides an opportunity for amazing ideas and concepts which would propel the business forward, and which would have otherwise gone undiscovered.

When your employees feel like their thoughts matter and their opinions are welcome, they will go to extra lengths to come up with worthy ideas that would help grow the business. In essence, they feel valued.

Active communication also gives a chance for employee encouragement. If employees bring up good ideas, they can be appreciated and encouraged. Even when they are doing good at their assigned task, you can promote their efforts.

As the leader of the business, it is up to you set the pace of communication among your workers.

If you duly communicate with your employees both in good and bad situations, it would serve as a guiding example to them as to how to communicate with each other.

Talking to them with respect and encouraging them always to communicate their thoughts on the business would lead them to do so; remember you create the ultimate example for actions among your staff.

Which brings me to business rapport.

Rapport refers to a close relationship whereby the parties understand each other's ideas, opinions, and feelings and communicate well. There is no better way to make your staff understand your plans and visions for the business than through a good business rapport.

Consistently communicating respectfully with and among your workers helps everyone develop mutual understanding; hence a good business rapport. In some organizations, not many words have to be said because a good business rapport exists.

There is a mutual understanding of everyone's feelings and thoughts towards the business, especially that of the business head, hence when things happen, everyone can individually tell if it is or is not suitable for the business because they are in tune with the common goal for the business.

A good business rapport helps your employees learn to work with their instincts which would be in tune with your wishes for the business, which in turn saves you time and energy not having to constantly explain how you want things to be done. Everyone around you should know and understand that already.

Here are some tricks which should form the basis of effective communication in your business:

- **Active listening:** Like I earlier implied, communication should be a two-way street. You should learn to be a good listener and not cultivate the habit of being the one to do all the speaking. Listening is the only way for you to hear the opinions and thoughts of the other party. Active listening is also a sign that you respect them enough to listen to what they have to say. Actively listen, that is, do not just let them speak but pay attention to what they are saying. That is the only way to get the gems in the communication--to get the meaning of any message Ask a related question if you're unclear or if you want the other party to elaborate further.

- **Getting criticism:** You have to accept that in communication, not everything you hear will be to your liking. Hence you have to build yourself up enough to be able to receive criticisms. Do not get defensive when a concept or work gets criticized but be open to understanding where the perspective of the person critiquing is coming from. Criticisms are not always a bad thing as that's the only way to know what you are not doing right so you can work towards bettering it.

    - **Giving criticism:** You will also need to criticize any of your employees' work if it is not up to par. Remember that you are both on the same side. To ensure that you do not bruise someone's feelings, do not make criticism persona. The best kind of work is done by people who do not feel diminished, so do not criticize the person but only his/her actions or work. Do not be condescending when critiquing. Talk about what you liked about the work or activity first, before you state the things you did not like or find to be subpar. Make sure also to appreciate the person giving his/her feedback for airing their thoughts and honest opinion to you.

- **Keep up:** This involves following up on a meaningful conversation you previously had. If something has already been critiqued and adjustments have been made, ask questions to make sure it was done right. Also, if you shared thoughts with an employee on actions to be taken, follow up to ensure that those actions have been made. A large part of communicating is following up. This is what gets the job done.

- **Trust:** Good communication stems from trust. Your employees have to have some level of confidence in you to be able to share their thoughts and opinions with you actively. So, it is not enough to promise that their views will be considered but to see to it that they are considered. Seeing their opinions and ideas (if they are up to par) effected will make them trust you enough to share their thoughts with you. Ensure honesty in every dealing and conversation as it is the right way to build trust. Make sure your actions match your words.

- **Balance:** Communication is vital and should be taken seriously. You have to strike a healthy balance in communicating with your employees and know where to draw the line between your leadership position and employees who try to control that with their attitudes. Use your instincts. Remember, you head the business, so when you hear thoughts and opinions, understand the perspective they are coming from and check with yourself to ensure they are in line with the vision you have for your business. Some thoughts might be valid for present times but do not work with the long-term goals you have set. Communicate that to employees so they know you have thought this through.

Transparency

In 2014, a survey carried out by the American Psychological Association showed that 25% of employees do not trust their employers.

Wow! That seems high coming from a founder and CEO perspective. I and the other management team have always strived for transparency. I don't think we have perfected transparency or communication to the company but hope that we have more that 75% of our employees' trust.

Transparency is a commonly misused word, and many now consider it cliché. Many business heads do not see the need to be open with employees since they do not answer to anyone. They believe this is the job of human resources.

However, this is typically not the case when it comes to startups. It may be years before the company grows large enough to warrant a full time HR person or department. Until then, that resposniblity falls to the management team.

It is safe to note that, while you head the business, you have a responsibility to those who work with you. You might not actively answer to them but your actions affect how they treat your business.

Transparency in business extends to all matters that affect your employees. Many organizations load secrets into contracts employees are made to sign, and many sign without reading. It makes no sense to bind an employee to a policy if they don't know what the policy is.

Ask employees to thoroughly read anything they are asked to sign to avoid getting trapped. These are mature individuals who have the right to know what's going on with their jobs. A happy employee goes a long way to making a successful business.

Transparency does not need to extend to your personal life or to sharing personal information about anyone in the company. However, personal antidotes help create a common bond with people, so don't be afraid to chat and expose your personal gains and failures.

How do you ensure transparency in your business?

- **Accept the risk:** Being transparent comes with certain risks. Employees should be able to easily access any information regarding the parts of the business that concerns them.. You might have to answer questions about areas they do not understand or the information you let out can be misused by some people. But this is all part of running a business, and this is just another good reason to screen employees carefully before hiring. You might even lose some employees because not everyone will be okay with the way things are being run, but note that it is in the best interest of your business in the long run. By being transparent you can also demand transparency in return.

- **Trust and honesty:** For you to choose to be transparent, you are deciding to trust the people you are dealing with, which is a big step. For you to be open, you also have to be honest since you will be asking for transparency in return. It's a lot easier for you to discover what employees are doing since everything is generally documented in their computer, and you should be able to see everything. But from your end, they should only be able to see what concerns them. if they're interested in financial reports, for example, and your company is public, they can access this information. If it's not public, they'll need to wait until the annual report comes out.

It is not enough, however, for information to be accessible. Information needs to be accurate and up to date. Everything should be documented and you should have no ulterior motives.

Authenticity: This may sound similar to honesty, but authenticity has more to do with you on a personal level. Don't hide behind an alter ego. Let employees know who you really are. Again, that doesn't mean you need to disclose personal information, just that you should show your true self so people will trust who you are.

The five benefits of transparency include:

1. It establishes trust between you and your employees and also you and your customers.
2. It fosters respect. When you and employees are transparent with each other, you will gain mutual respect.
3. It builds long-lasting relationships. Relationships formed on the right foundation are healthy and long-lasting. The scope of

your business relationship will be expanded with more meaningful conversations in the right direction. Even after they stop working for you, you will still have a good relationship with them.

4. It improves productivity. People tend to thrive in genuine environments. When there are no secrets, employees know who and what they are working with and act accordingly.
5. It improves innovation. By being transparent, the strengths and weaknesses of every worker will be easier to identify. Knowing their strengths, the right tasks can be put their way. In today's business world, innovation is strengthen. Transparency gives employees the freedom to innovate within the parameters of their position, and you may discover that you have hit on a genius in your hiring who happens to come up with a world-changing idea that would have gone unnoticed without this freedom. It can also give you insight into possible problems as well as open ground for new ideas and solutions.

It is safe to say that transparency is an investment in your business. The workplace becomes a safe ground where every individual knows what is at stake.

Good employees will easily work in the right direction and thrive in their areas of endeavor.

As the business head and leader, transparency projects you as confident enough to put the cards on the table, one who is sure enough to make the right decisions, and it shows.

Business And Pleasure

Differentiating between business and pleasure is a very tricky aspect of relationship-building in business. It is easy to cross the line and forget it is business.

While you want everyone to have a good business rapport, you do not want them to slack in their jobs; hence it is necessary to enforce some steps to balance things out.

You're firstly their boss, not their friend. You can be friendly, but you're not their peer. You're their leader. This distinction is important when everyone starts to get carried away during working hours. It's okay to talk and have some fun as long as the work does not suffer.

If the room becomes unfocused, that is the time for you to step in as the leader and gently ensure everyone returns to the original focus; getting work down.

Ways to do that include:

1. **Switching tones from playful to serious.** Your voice tone does a lot to communicate your thoughts.
2. **Ensure that conversations stay on topic.** Deviation will arise, but make sure you direct the conversation back to topic. When someone deviates into something off focus, speak up and bring him or her back in line.
3. **Enforce dress codes:** Formal dress codes are not a must, and many creative and tech companies allow employees to "dress down". But there's a fine line between wearing jeans and a tee shirt and wearing dirty, ripped clothes, gang colors, derogatory graphic tees, flip flops, or other clothing that is meant for the gym or the beach.

    In offices where vendors or clients have access, clean and neat is the way to go. Suits can be reserved for the C-suite, but other employees should wear business casual or higher, depending on the area of your business; whatever they wear should suit work.
4. **Know when to reprimand an employee.** Never hold back reprimands when an employee is blatantly out of conduct as silence is often mistaken for consent.

So, when an employee is throwing caution to the wind, ensure to speak against it. Do this privately, not in front of other employees. This is the ideal time to allow employees to voice their grievances and feelings. If another employee is implicated, speak to that employee alone.

If stories conflict, get them together with you to sort out the truth. Be sure to keep a log of all reprimands stating exactly what the infraction is. Have the employee sign it and date it and give them a copy for their personal file. That way there will be no surprises when and if they are eventually let go due to continued reprimands.

Mixing business with pleasure can have adverse effects on your business and often conflicts with your vision.

Make sure to separate the two in the workplace. Outside the workplace, it's best not to socialize with employees with the exception of company sanctioned events, such as team building exercises or a company picnic, for example.

Your employees will naturally build their own culture within the workplace, and will obviously develop closer relationships with their peers, but it's your job to ensure that they carry out their tasks and activities in line with your business policies.

Building good business relationships is essential in ensuring that everyone does their best work. Using the various trick and tips shared in these chapters, building healthy sound relationships with employees should be as easy as talking.

Chapter Nine: Economic Affairs

"When money realizes that it is in good hands, it wants to stay and multiply in those hands."
~Idowu Koyenikan

The subject of money is always a delicate issue, business not excluded. For some reason, we've been hard-wired to not talk about it, to keep our finances secret, to not let others know anything about our money. But if you are ignorant about your finances, you'll have less chance of making more of the stuff.

In businesses, monetary affairs will pose problems until you have a grasp on how money works. So, as a business owner with the mind to make a profit, you need to fully understand your business's money and money issues.

There is a relationship between leadership and money, as proper money management is a leadership skill.

Sounds silly?

There's a direct correlation between people who properly manage their money how they control and organize their lives.

People who take charge of their lives know exactly how much money they have, how they've spent their money, and how much they will need in at least the immediate future.

Isn't that also part of leadership?

I know what you might be thinking; you are not a finance guru or accountant or anything like that.

Why should you be bothered about the financial aspect of your company?

Everyone should be, first and foremost, their own account officer or finance officer before anyone else.

Your business is a part of you and falls under the classification of your affairs, so you need to take charge of its pecuniary affairs too.

Let's explore monetary, or pecuniary, affairs.

Pecuniary refers to *relating to or involving money*; that is, monetary award, monetary interest, money in general--how it's obtained and how it's used.

Affairs, on the other hand, refers to *matters or issues of something*.

Pecuniary affairs refer to money related matters or issues involving money.

As a leaderpreneur, how do you handle the monetary affairs of your business?

How do you handle the relationship between leadership and money?

Don't worry, the subsequent parts of this chapter will reveal all you need to know.

LEADERSHIP and MONEY

As a leader, you have a significant role to play in maximizing opportunities to turn in more money for your business. You have to leverage the products and services your business has to offer to make money.

Aside from the business making profit, you would need to manage these monies to ensure proper financial growth. How do I mean? It is not enough for the business to make a profit, but for the profit to be adequately utilized in order to grow the business. And as the leader of the business, you are at the forefront of making this happen.

Here are some necessary steps to take to ensure this.

- **BUSINESS ACCOUNT:** A lot of business owners, especially small business owners, underemphasize the need for a business account. If your business is registered under the law, it is an entity of its own and should be treated as such. Running your business under your personal account is detrimental to the business's growth because accountability is not ensured. And you may find yourself in trouble down the road with taxes.

    With a business account strictly used for the business's monetary affairs, it is easier to track what comes in and what goes out and properly take account. Your credits and debits can easily be accounted for if they're properly documented.

Most people don't do this by hand anymore. We live in the information age and every business has access to computer technology and finance software to do the accounting work for you. All you need to do is input information.

This way, you can take account at the end of the month for expenses, profits, and other financial statuses.

Having a working business account is also beneficial in building the credit score of that business.

Think long term; if you need to take a loan to secure a business expansion or fund more significant projects, a well-managed business account can work in your favor.

Banks check the account history of any account before dishing out loans, and some even give preferences to business accounts for business loans.

So, you need to set up a business account.

Ensure the account is used to handle every financial affair of the business, from the purchase of raw materials to payment of staff, petty cash, and everything else. Use only the business credit card associated with your business account for business-related expenses. A business account is an excellent start to proper business financial management.

- **ACCOUNTABILITY:** Accountability refers to taking responsibility for tasks, behavior, performance, and so on. Concerning business, accountability involves adequately accounting for every aspect of the business.

In handling monetary affairs, one needs to ensure the utmost level of accountability.

As the leader of the business, you need proper documentation for every financial involvement of business like:

- **Budget:** Every financially smart individual knows that proper budgeting is a leading financial requirement. This is the first step in accountability. You need to inculcate this in your business. For every product or service to be rendered, a budget should be done for the cost price of either the goods or services, everything from quantity, type of inputs or materials, depreciation, storage, labor, utilities, and anything else that is relevant to building goods and services.

   The price of everything must be calculated and documented. Also, allow an additional five percent in your budget for miscellaneous, which is basically for anything that does not fall under any purchase category or to cover an unplanned expense that might come up during purchase. The five percent is taken from the total budget before you add miscellaneous expenses.

   With proper budgeting, you always know where money was spent. It also helps to caution spending and keeps the purchasing in check.

- **Receipts:** Receipts are evidence of payment. They can be hard copy slips of paper or received as a document online.

Always collect the receipts for any purchase incurred by the business. This would be used to ensure that the prices put down under cost or expenses are correct. It would help to ensure accountability and honesty among you and your staff. Let every purchase be accounted for through the receipts. Make it a standing rule that receipts of any business-related purchase are kept.

(Many apps already exist for connecting directly to credit card accounts for easy receipt/reimbursement management. Try to go paperless as it will make your life much easier!)

This also helps to reduce stealing in the business, and perhaps most importantly, you're expenses can be verified by the IRS when it comes to tax time.

- **Personal loans to the business:** As the head of the business, the business might need external funding, and you might offer that external funding.

  This is not always the best idea, but if you find it's necessary, keep an accurate record of any of these kinds of loans to your business. Write a personal check from a personal account as though you are an investor.

  Like I said before, treat the business as its own entity.

  Do not look at this as "both the business's money and my personal money are mine, so there is no need for a distinction."

A proper accounting distinction is fundamental and essential.

If you don't make these distinctions, you can not fully track the business's cash inflow and whether the business is making a profit or loss.

This is also an essential aspect of accountability.

Once again, you will find yourself in deep trouble during tax time. Your personal finances will be subject to business taxes, you will have no proof that you "loaned" the business money, and you may receive penalties for nondisclosure.

- **FINANCIAL DECISIONS:** This is a critical aspect of the pecuniary affairs of your business, just as it is one of the crucial aspects of leadership.

  You need to understand that when running a business, you need adequate knowledge of certain key areas, of which finance is one part.

  The excuse of not being "finance personnel" does not cut it. You will need to make vital financial decisions, and you have to be prepared for it.

  Here are some tips for financial decisions:

1. **Do not overstress the business.** A typical killer of many businesses is financial/debt overload. Everyone wants their business to be enough to pay their bills and sort out their lifestyle, but this can only be the case if you give the business space to grow.

   For this to happen, stay in line with the profit of the business. Pay yourself a salary instead of taking money when you need it. This goes back to mixing personal and business accounts. Taking a salary is beneficial to your business tax liability.

   Reinvest remaining profit back into the business to bring about growth. Pay yourself as little as you can, this way you can set aside money for other things like unexpected expenses a.k.a emergency funds. Do not forget that the growth of the business depends on these things.

   Making the mistake of piling all your personal financial burdens on the business and/or overspending on supplies when it starts bringing profit will kill the business fast. Avoid financial overload on the business, be patient, and let the business grow well enough to accommodate your numerous expenses and needs.

2. **Emergency funds:** This is an often-forgotten necessity. As your business grows, set aside money for emergency occurrences. This way, the business does not have to suffer from downtime when something goes wrong.

   Your printer or phone system might break down, the cost of goods might go up, or you may incur unexpected expenses due to things like workplace safety.

Every month take out money to be saved ahead of emergency occurrences. Anything can happen, and you want to be prepared for it. You want your business to continue to run in spite of any unexpected setbacks.

3. **Outsource:** When running a business, your first thought might be to have all the personnel you need to run the business on board from the start/ You want to have fast access to any required skill. But hiring enough permanent people to do everything you need will cost you, perhaps more than you need to spend in the beginning.

   Instead, try to outsource skills that are not regularly required. A legal advisor is a good example of personnel that can be outsourced. Instead of having one on the payroll, opt for one you can pay only when you need his/her services--on a per-task basis.

4. **Expansion:** Every business owner wants his/her business to grow and expand. However, it is vital to note that there is something called premature expansion. Before you decide to expand, make sure that you have outgrown your current size. Do not just make this decision from one month of excesses, but keep track of profit/loss over a period of twelve months or more to make sure it is really needed.

   From the first time you notice that expansion might be needed, start thinking about it, planning for it, and saving towards it. Your decision to expand should not have a severe financial impact on the business all at once; save money needed for this over time.

In fact, it's always a good idea to begin saving for this from the start. After all, you probably already know that at some point you're going to want to grow the company. By planning ahead, you'll be ready to expand when you are sure you need it.

In the rare case where a company is so hot that they experience a surge of sales and popularity before they're ready to expand, they may not be able to fulfill orders. This is something you might consider preparing for also. Go to lenders for the financial boost you need. If you have so many orders or requests for your product or service that you can't fulfill them (preorders), and they're documented, this is as good as cash to any lender. Show them your documentation and they'll likely give you a loan.

5. **Loans:** An easy mistake many business owners make is waiting for things to deteriorate before seeking loans or lines of credit. They keep hoping something will turn around. But most times, when things go bad, it's too late to request a loan.

   The business's finances will have taken a turn for the worse, making you less eligible for loans. Look into getting loans or lines of credit before you need them. Don't wait until things get bad.

   You can also use loans to finance expansions or large projects. Loans are not always bad except when you are not able to pay them back, but if they are well planned out, they can be a blessing to the business.

   The general rule, which seems counter-intuitive, is to always use someone else's money, not your own, to run your business.

The more good credit you have, the more likely it will be that people will loan you more money (of course, within your business's earning potential).

6. **Seek help:** When you are not sure about how to handle specific issues, seek help from people who have better knowledge. Do not cover your problem until they get out of hand. Once you notice an issue where you feel out of your depth, seek help immediately through resources such as classes or seminars, books, online guidance, mentors, you're business's legal counsel or other business owners.

CONTROL OF FINANCIAL MATTERS

As I mentioned earlier, as a business leader, you would need to take control of the business's financial matters, but you should always be aware of its status.

To adequately take control of this crucial area of your business, you need to prepare yourself to step into this role by gaining the knowledge needed.

While finance might not be your strong point or be related to your course of study, you need to acquire basic knowledge in this area for the sake of your business.

Personally, I recommend reading up on fundamental aspects of finance in business, and if you can afford to, take a course on it. This would go a long way to prepare you for the task ahead; it would broaden your knowledge on the concepts of finance and teach you the basic finance skills needed.

The pecuniary affairs of your business are delicate and critical, and should be treated as such; here proper knowledge is king. No one can afford to make mistakes when it comes to money--losing money.

So, establish strategies to ensure financial growth. The financial matters of the business run across profit and loss, expenses, cost price, cost of labor, and so on, so you need to know enough about these distinct areas to tackle them. Don't forget to include your business's physical location; ensure it is within the business budget.

If you cannot afford to take a space alone, share with another business that offers a different but related kind of product or service. For example, if you run a salon, you can share the space with a nail technician or make-up artist. This would even boost your own business as their customers are also your potential customers and vice versa, so a win-win situation.

There are several companies, such as ADP and Rippling, for example, that will handle your payroll, with easy online access by you. All you need to do is input employee information. Employees will have a portal where they can view just their own pay status. These companies handle everything from sales taxes to payroll taxes and all Federal government yearly requirements.

Create a profitability timeline. With a detailed list of the expenses incurred in setting up your business and other close future expenses, use it to plan your profitability timeline. This will give you a concrete idea of what you need to work toward.

I also recommend that, as a founder, you plan your profitability timeline to include enough money to cover your personal expenses until you get to the point where you can take a steady paycheck.

Be sure to document everything you can that might be covered by the business. For example, if you work from home, these are deductions that would legally be allowed. Certain auto expenses, utilities, meetings, and even clothes are things you can look into that might be covered.

Do not hesitate to cut down on unnecessary costs wherever you can.

It is easy to make initial mistakes when setting up for your business, but once you realize an unnecessary cost or expense, adjust.

This is also counter-intuitive. I've told you to create a plan and stick to it, but you also need to be flexible. If something isn't working, cut it.

Keep in mind, efforts to trim the fat, streamline processes, and create business efficiencies is not a one-time thing. Remember to periodically review expenses, re-negotiate vendor contracts, and other housekeeping tasks to ensure you are maximizing your net profits!

As an example, you might have purchased some equipment with the view that you needed it, and you might have needed it at the time, but if it's served its purpose you can sell it. If you think you might need it again in the future, lease it out on a monthly basis until you need it.

Channel the money you receive into a more critical aspect of the business. To cut down on costs, you can also look into buying preloved (used) items that are in good condition.

If you want to manufacture great tee shirts, for example, purchase used industrial machines. These are workhorses that rarely wear out. If you're a tech company, used keyboard, desks, and chairs are the way to go.

Remember, the goal is to grow the business, focusing on that goal, and managing current situations until you have a solid foundation.

Earlier in the chapter, I talked about budgeting and taking account. If you're not ready to hire an accountant or finance personnel, an excellent way to go about these important tasks is to make use of software designed to track expenditures, create budgets, and do accounting.

A big plus with software and applications is that they're mobile; your budgets or accounts are accessible from anywhere, so they're at your fingertips whenever and wherever you're making purchases: wholesalers, trade shows, or unexpected sales that might pop up.

You can also share access to these platforms with your accountants as you scale the business. This will make life easier as tax time approaches as you'll want professional help to get the year-end closed.

Have a good financial strategy. To effectively manage the business's finances, create strategies for handling financial details.

For example, choose a bill-paying method that is in the best interest of the business, such as monthly auto-pay for utilities which can be averaged based on the past year's usage, or quarterly tax payments if your business is eligible.

If paying your taxes quarterly is not working, consider spreading the payment out monthly, so it becomes like every other monthly expense.

You can also include rent in your monthly expenses if you have a physical shop, or you might to pay a six-month lease, for example, all at once.

A financial strategy to keep clients paying on time is one of the most important aspects of keeping your business in the black.

You can give incentives to clients who pay on time to encourage others to follow suit. A two percent discount on their bill can go a long way to incentivize people.

Implement different means of making payments so clients can choose their method of getting money to you: ACH, payment apps, PayPal or CashApp, check, major credit card, directly online, phone-in, and so on.

Also, monitor the financial strengths and weaknesses of your business. Different businesses have periods where they do better in sales.

There are seasons, months, and specific occasions that are more favorable to certain businesses than others. Use that knowledge to your advantage.

For example, if you're in retail, your business sells a lot during February due to Valentine's Day, or Mother's Day, or Christmas. Plan to offset major bills during that period. Use whatever period your business thrives best to your financial advantage.

The only way to really be in control of your company and its finances is to get involved; know your company's financial status at all times like you know the back of your hand.

HANDLING PROFIT AND LOSS WITH LEADERSHIP SKILL

This is a rather exciting area of the financial affairs of the business. Profit and loss always seem like the most straightforward financial concept to understand.

But understanding profit and loss is not the task; the task is how you handle it. What do you do with the business after knowing whether you are making a profit or loss?

- **PROFIT:** This simply refers to financial gain over and above expenses. It is when the money earned is more than the money spent. Profit is the goal of every business.

A profit or loss statement is one of the significant financial statements used to check the business's strength and growth.

Every business, aside from non-profit organizations, is set up with the aim of making a profit. However, it is one thing to make a profit, and it is another thing to manage profits adequately.

Hence the following tips:

1. An improvement in the profit margin of your business should not be equated with immediate extra money to your income.

    It is very easy to get carried away when your business is making profit, and, as mentioned, this should be tracked over a period of time to identify whether profit is a seasonal spurt or anomaly, or a steady trend in sales.

2. When profit is consistent, keep growth in mind; add a sensible percentage to your personal income and add the remaining

profit to the business's capital to ensure growth.

3. Allow profits to push you to do more; do not settle for keeping the company stagnant; once you start earning profits, continue to think of ways to improve your product or service, your efficiency, your costs, and your production processes.

- **LOSS:** This is the opposite of profit. It is when the money spent is more than the profit earned.

Nobody wishes this for their business, but certain situations can contribute to this.

The 2019 coronavirus pandemic caused many businesses to fail, and those who were able to make it through saw a loss in sales.

Any business that had an online sales presence had a greater chance of maintaining their sales, and some even saw an increase. However, COVID-19 was a global pandemic that temporarily crippled much of the world's economy.

Many businesses scrambled to make deeper cost-cutting measures to sustain the business during the slow down. These cuts came in the form of layoffs, furloughs, contract re-negotiations, and scaling back on R&D spending just to name a few.

The bottom line is this: when you experience a loss in your business, do the following:

1. Do not take any impulsive action first.

2. Go back to your books and assess the situation. Check when sales started depreciating.

3. Discuss with key members of your business and try to find out the problem.

4. Cut down on expenses for the meantime to fill the gap left by the loss.

5. Think about ways to improve the situation. You might need to make some tweaks in your long-term plan; improve on your product or service, and whatever the business seemingly needs.

6. Take measures to avoid making the same mistake that caused the loss in the first place.

7. Seek external help if need be. A financial advisor might make a lot of difference. You might need to take a loan or line of credit to finance the changes you want to make to the business. An advisor might also help you pinpoint what went wrong or how you can reduce costs in manufacturing, for example.

A loss does not have to signal the end of the business; it is more like a wake-up call.

So, do not think of it as something you cannot move on from. Also, refrain from transferring blame; instead, focus on making improvements.

Remember, having full knowledge at all times of the pecuniary affairs of your business is critical to keeping your business advancing, particularly in times of downturn; you need adequate knowledge.

Monitor your books, get familiar with the finances of your business, its strengths and weaknesses, know your way around financial concepts, make friends with accountants, and make the best financial decisions.

With finances, knowledge is king!

Chapter Ten: Augmentation

"Be undeniably good. No marketing effort or social media buzzword can be a substitute for that."
~**Anthony Volodkin, founder of Hype Machine**

Augmentation refers to the process of making something more prominent in size or amount. In business, augmentation refers to the process of improving the size and scope of the business. In short, it's the expansion or growth of a business.

The ultimate task of augmentation is vested on you, as this falls within your purview as the administrator of the business.

Augmenting the business would require you to take up the task of a rainmaker, and bring in opportunities for expansion.

In this chapter, I'll be explaining the process of augmentation in a business and how to go about it.
To help you navigate this weighing task, the different areas to cover, and the processes involved, I'll break down the different aspects involved.

The goal is to equip you with the knowledge of how to carry out this task, not just as the administrator of the business but as a leader.

EXPANSION

As the leader of a business, you are also the rainmaker. You are charged with the responsibility of generating income for the business.

I know it is a lot of responsibility, but you founded a startup knowing it would be work, right?

While this is not an easy task to regularly carry out, you bracing up and taking up the challenge is a good enough way to start.

- **EXPANDING TERRITORIES LIKE A LEADER.**

    While everyone who owns a business likes the idea of growing, not everyone can take risk expansion.

    For any business with long term plans, growth is necessary; you have to grow to keep up with customers' needs.

    This does not change the fact that, for business owners, growth and choice of expansion is a risk they should take, and this is not easy.

    This is why it is necessary to make these choices carefully because a premature expansion can kill a business. With the knowledge of this necessary evil for business owners, you need a foolproof strategy to ensure you are on track.

    Now down to the topic: How do you expand your territories like a leader?

    Firstly, it is essential to understand why leadership should be a driving force when building your territories. As a leader, you have adequate information about the business, from its goals, mission, and visions to its strengths and weaknesses and a host of other relevant information. With this knowledge, you should have an idea of the kind of people you need for the business and just about everything else the business needs.

The expansion involves a lot of strategizing, planning, and understanding. You are not just opening your business to more prominent spaces and tasks, but you're also capitalizing on the business's strengths.

Knowledge of the business's primary needs in terms of resources (which can be people, materials, money, time), you can now be guided as to how you go about getting them—knowing what the business needs would serve as a direction on how to get these needs.

So as the leader of the business, you are to carry everyone--all key personnel--along on decisions and plans. With an expansion in mind, you work with your employees to discover the needs of the business as well as the strong points to capitalize on during the process.

You are also thinking up means to improve the weaker aspects of the business to meet the requirements or standards of the expansion.

Expansion doesn't happen in a bubble. Thus, leadership is important because there will need to be assignments made, data tracked, and other collaborative items that need a leader.

Now that we understand why leadership is a prerequisite for the expansion, let's move on to the plan.

The first line of approach on the process of expansion after deducing the business's needed resources is *networking*.

The journey of expanding your business territories involves getting the much-needed resources externally, either in the form of skill sets, clientele, or funds. Networking is a great way to find people who can help you support and grow your business.

- **NETWORKING**

    Networking refers to expanding your contacts by interacting with others and exchanging information.

    It is a form of linking where you exchange information and ideas with people you share a common interest with or for a particular interest.

    Often, these are people you did not initially know personally. It is trying to meet people who might be relevant and useful in your endeavors.

    Networking commonly occurs in places or events of common interest, but you can network anywhere. Wherever there are people, you may find a networking opportunity. Keep an open mind.
    It also goes beyond meeting these people; it involves keeping active communication with them for mutual benefits.

Networking is a common way to meet people who could be relevant in getting the much-needed resources for your expansion.

The expansion should not be an impulsive decision. It involves time, planning and strategizing. You should always be networking so that when you do decide to expand, you'll have contacts in place.
During consideration and building a strategy is the period when you should be extending yourself to contacts who might be of any help in the expansion process.

The point of networking is not to leech onto these people for help, support, or resources but to find people who can be instrumental in your entrepreneurship journey. They might have access to the help you need during expansion. And when and if the times comes that they need you, you'll need to be there for them as well.

- **NEW MARKETS**

    The idea of expansion is growth and more exposure, and an excellent way to go about this is to find a new market, get in and dominate it.

    How do you penetrate new markets?

    How do you gain the attention of a new market?

    What marketing techniques should you use?

    Gaining a new market means expanding to new territories.

That's where you'll find a new set of customers and an improved customer base. Review the areas currently getting your products and determine why these people buy from you, then seek out new areas with the same demographic where you can spread your business.

If you have decided to expand into a new market, how do you want to go about your introduction to the new market?

What should your advertising technique be or what marketing strategy should you implement?

You need to create a new marketing plan, one that first introduces your company and its products or services to get people familiar with your brand.

Once you pass your brand message to the new market, you can begin to systematically go through all the marketing techniques to conquer the new market, including affiliate marketing, generating traffic to your site, social media, surveys, email blasts, blogs, and improving sales copy.

Tap into the sales or delivery channel; this way, you can benefit from online opportunities.

Keep in mind, an expansion may not only be a physical presence. Expansion may be in the form of opening a new sales verticle that requires the same type of analysis minus some of the costs, such as physical office space.

- **ADD NEW PRODUCTS**

This seems like a basic principle, but it is gold. If you run a business where you offer products, you can add more products to your line, especially if your primary products are doing well. Find out what your customers need or what is an excellent complimentary product to your original product.

Also, conduct market research to ensure what people need and the price range they are willing to pay for such a product. This should be done before you commit any form of resources to the idea just to make sure that you are on track.

Your market research will reveal what people want, and this would guide your product choice and approach.

- **LEGALITIES**

If you are sure that your business is ready for expansion, then this is the right time to get legal help. Before you buy that land for your proposed office site, for example, consult your attorney (and you're accountant if you have one). If your business was so small that you did not even register it under the law, this is an excellent time to register it.

Whatever decisions you are making, make sure they are legally viable by seeking legal advice.

- **RE-BRANDING**

If you have had previous discomforts about how your business has been branded, this is a perfect time to make a change--before you expand into new markets.

Expansion is a good time to reintroduce yourself to the world of business.

With the knowledge you have gained from experience, you should decide what changes to make to your brand's identity. So, get feedback from your staff and know the message you want to portray. This is the time to correct any wrong idea you might have previously passed out about your business.

- **GET LOCAL**

    Expansion can make you lose touch with your immediate environment. You can get so absorbed in entering a new market and dominating new industries that you forget to pay attention to your primary environment and customer base.

    This is an excellent time to gain their attention, be part of or sponsor events within your locality. Target the local media and have a reliable public relations strategy to win them over. Hand feed them the talking points you want them to relay to the public. Don't leave it to their interpretation. When choosing which events to take part in, look out for events geared toward your target audience.

    For instance, if you are a hair brand, look out for events geared toward women. If you're a tech company, get involved in events where young people are likely to attend. Book a stand or be part of the sponsorship; just get involved with the process and use the opportunity to sell your brand.

    Make sure you offer all your contact information and where to buy in any printed handouts, banners, or freebies. Your logo and website should be on everything.

If you decide to use influencers, keep in touch with your local base by picking some people around your locality who have a proven following.

- **EMBRACE THE IDEA**

If an expansion is something is you think the business is ready for, then
embrace the idea and everything that comes with it. It will require dedication, possibly longer work hours, and will likely interfere with your personal life to some degree, even if only temporarily. You need to be ready to accept this as part of growing and expanding your business. Accept tasks look at everything as a new challenge. With a welcoming mindset, you should do well.

If an expansion is something is you think the business is ready for, then embrace the idea and everything that comes with it. It will require dedication, possibly longer work hours, and will likely interfere with your personal life to some degree, even if only temporarily. You need to be ready to accept this as part of growing and expanding your business. Accept tasks look at everything as a new challenge. With a welcoming mindset, you should do well.

Remember, nothing good comes easily. So, take the process of growth as part of the journey to being a better company.

Also, ensure that your workers are bringing their A-game to the process. You should have already explained to your employees your decision to expand the business, and they should understand that this is going to possibly be quite trying for everyone involved. Impress upon them that this should be seen as a way to better the company.

The right mindset is necessary for such a process. The universe is attracted to the energy you put out, so positivity from everyone will bring great results.

BRANDING

In a preceding chapter, I explained that your business is its own entity and should be treated as such. You cannot go into business without associating yourself with something, so we need to talk at length about branding.

Your brand represents the guiding principles of your company. When someone sees your brand, it signifies the qualities they're looking for, so, it is not enough to simply connect with the right customers, they need to know that you stand behind what your brand represents--that your product consistently gives them whatever it is you've declared yourself to stand for. This is how people decide who to buy from, and it's where brand loyalty starts.

If you're discovered dealing with the wrong ideologies, principles that don't correspond with your company's vision and mission, customers will quickly pick up on that. We live in the information age, and there's really no way to hide what you're doing, for the most part.

Which leads to this question, the vital question you must ask yourself as your first step in your plan to create a startup: what do you want to stand for?

What ideologies do you support or disregard?

How will you differentiate yourself among all the other companies doing the same thing?

These questions are essential to ensure proper branding. And it should be personal. Don't try to "read" the market or second-guess what people want. You must decide what *you* want. That's the only way you'll remain passionate about your business. It must represent *you*.

Brands are easily associated with what that company stands for, which can work for or against them. And that's not a bad thing. It simply means that customers quickly know who they want to buy from based on their knowledge of that brand.

Your brand should be distinct with some sort of personality, or it will get lost in the sea of other businesses. Your brand is essentially your business's identity--something people can instantly associate with your product or service. And within your niche, you must decide whether your product is a luxury brand, a premium brand, and so on. This is all going to be part of your market research. You need to decide who is going to be most likely to want or need your products or services.

UNDERSTANDING YOUR MARKET

Don't decide on a name for your business until you first understand your market. A successful marketing plan includes picking a target audience--who you want to be associated with and who will most likely want to be associated with you.

And this involves excelling in the following areas:

- **Communicating the right story**: This involves the messages you portray as a company--how you tell your story.

    Story sells because people want to identify with what that story represents. Marketing and sales is more about emotionally connecting with people and how they want to see their lives rather than hard-line tactics.

    The actions you take as a business should reflect your story.

    For example, if you want to take a stand for or against a social movement such as Black Lives Matter, Save the Whales, Gay Rights, Anti-War, Right to Life, or any other social movement, be sure this is something you feel strongly about because you may lose customers.

    You will also gain customers, and those customers are likely to remain loyal to your brand. Never just casually link yourself to a social movement or cause because you think it's the popular thing to do.

    Deviating from your core mission and brand story will cause you to get off message and can confuse your following--your customer base. The way businesses react to these issues is just to track their behavior. Only then can you decide if this is something you want to associate with or not.

- In communicating your story, you'll likely be using social media, email blasts, events, and other means.

  You must be intentional about every post you put out because they represent your brand, the company's culture, and the company's voice.

  You want your message to be clear, not subject to subjective interpretation, which is something people are prone to do. What you say directly influences how people view your brand.

  Everything should align with your brand's core mission.

  Every aspect of your brand identity from your name, logo, adverts, influencer choices, packaging, and so on should resonate with the brand identity you seek to create. You cannot call yourself a luxury brand and not invest in your packaging, for example, and the quality of customers' experience.

- **Standing out from the competition**: Every business has its unique journey, and it is easy to get carried away when you're trying to differentiate yourself from the pack, especially if you're in a strongly competitive industry such as tech or clothing.

  Do not imitate other brands or copy their branding style because it takes away originality.

  Focus on telling your own story and passing your message, do not get caught up in watching competitors so tightly that you gradually make changes that you would not typically have made.

- **Targeting the right audience:** You have created a product or service, you've formed your mission statement--your values and what you and your company stand for--and you have a good idea about which demographic you want to target.

    While your business involves providing a product or service, there's no point in an excellent product or service with no one to offer it to.

    How can what you have to offer be seen and accepted? How does the business establish a purpose in the eyes of the public, your potential customers?

    The answer to all these questions is people, the right people.

    Yes, the right people, the adjective *right* is essential there.

    People might surround you, but only the right set can make things happen. Now, this is where you come in as the leader and rainmaker, getting these right people. And for this, you might require the assistance of a marketing staff.

    For you to fully take charge of the business, you have to somehow provide the clientele, maybe just for the initial bump, then the referrals that come off that based on the precedent of good work can take up the work for you. So how do you achieve getting the clients or customer base for your business?

    Every business should know its target audience--its potential customer base.

To understand this, you'll need to undertake an in-depth demographic analysis to understand the age, sex, race, income, spending habits, living arrangement, family composition, and so on of a specific population.

Find out what these sets of people are interested in--where and how often do they currently shop, what do they look for, how much do they spend each month on non-essentials, for example. Once you decide who your target market is, use that information to develop your marketing strategies.
You must initially focus on a specific generally narrow target audience, or you won't be able to hone in on the direction to take with marketing, advertisement, and any strategy.

Very few companies appeal to a broad market that covers almost all demographics. These brands might include Apple, Amazon, Coke or Pepsi products, and other big names like that.

Your branding strategy is the blueprint for how you plan to go about getting your message out. Once you have identified who your first market Is going to be, you need to map out a strategy around that audience, or the strategy is useless.

Never forget that a brand is a business's most valuable asset, so tread carefully with it. It is okay to look to other brands for inspiration but don't get lost in what they do.

Ensure you understand the kind of brand you are seeking to create and who your ideal customer is, then let that guide your actions.

TOP LEADERSHIP AND MANAGEMENT SKILLS

When dealing with augmentation, there is a line that crosses between leadership and management. You'll be wearing two hats: managing the business through this period effectively, leading--carrying everyone along on the journey to expansion.

Business augmentation requires some level of dedication from everybody involved in the business process. While you are the manager ensuring that everyone is doing their job and getting things done in a timely manner, make sure your staff is well compensated for the efforts.

As the business head, during the process of expansion, you would need to exhibit the following skills.

- **COMMUNICATION:** Communication is being mentioned again because it crosses all areas of running a business from creating a plan to a public startup, building a team, augmentation, marketing, and everything else.

   This is a period that calls for active and honest communication with your staff. No one is a mind reader, so you speak up about any new direction or actions you've decided to take and how you expect things to be handled during that process.

   You need to adequately express yourself to your workers and give them the chance to do the same. Listen to their suggestions through this process and acknowledge their efforts. This is a time when everyone should come together to work for the future of the brand.

- **INTEGRITY:** During this process, your integrity will be regularly tested, but you have to stick to your values and keep the brand's mission in mind. Do not jeopardize everything your business stands for to take advantage of a quick opportunity. Another better opportunity will come along, one in which you will not have to lower your standards or compromise your integrity. Without integrity, no real success is possible.

    Integrity will make you an excellent leader and reflects in simple actions like taking responsibility for your mistakes, giving credit where due, and being appreciative of your employees' time and effort.

- **EMPATHY:** This will also be tested a lot during this period because while you are so focused on growing your brand, you will naturally expect your workers to be as dedicated to this task as you are.

    However, your employees have a life outside of work, so they might not be able to commit a hundred percent like you are, and you have to allow for that. While demanding the best from them, you would need to cut them some slack.

- **VISION:** This should be a driving force for you through this period. Allow the vision you have for your business to guide your decisions.

"Good business leaders create a vision, articulate the vision, passionately own the vision, and relentlessly drive it to completion."
~Jack Welch

With these skills, I am sure you are ready for the leadership task of expansion.

11

Conclusion

All your dreams can come true if you have the courage to pursue them.
~Walt Disney

This has been a journey through understanding the fusion of entrepreneurship and leadership. There is no exact recipe for success; however, there are guidelines and footpaths from people who have walked the road of success.

In the past, the role of leadership in entrepreneurship was underemphasized.

The general assumption was that entrepreneurial skills naturally encompassed leadership skills, and although this is certainly possible with some, it's not the norm. That's another reason why so many startups fail.

Lack of leadership allows for too many variables to enter the picture and is a leading cause of entrepreneurs straying from their original plan.

Taking charge of your business and stepping up to responsibilities goes a long way in growing your business. But just because you may have the courage of your convictions, doesn't mean you know where to start, how to go about it, and what you might be doing wrong.

It is paramount to summarize the tips and knowledge shared in this book to conclude this journey through leaderpreneurship. Each chapter had its gems and takeaways.

In the book, I revealed the secrets of the jungle (business world) and how to navigate that world.

Standards are not classified basically by the amount of money spent in the process, but the entire process, the choices you make, how you handle the process, and everything else in between.

In summary, here are the rules and takeaways you should embrace in your mission to be the best in your industry.:

Rule #1: Strive to make a profit. That's why you're in business.

Rule #2: Offer value. If you can't compete in price, compete in value.

Rule #3: Solve a problem or find a solution. Can you innovate an existing product or find a better way to do something?

Rule #4: Adopt the right mindset. The mind has a powerful way of attracting things that are in harmony with it, both positive and negative, and for you to effectively utilize the power of your mind, you need to develop and train it.

In his book *Wealth for All: Living a Life of Success at the Edge of Your Ability"* internationally recognized business consultant Idowu Koyenikan tells us that the mind is just like a muscle; the more you exercise it, the stronger it gets and can be expanded. The dreams you are working to achieve need both the work and the right mindset to make it happen. So, do not underestimate the power of your mind.

Rule #5: Always start with a plan. Creating your business is like bringing an idea to life, and planning is the only way to ensure that the specs and details are on par with the initial idea you had for the business.

Rule #6: Stick to your mission and your budget. You need to note tips like not compromising your integrity, doing things economically, having emergency funds, and staying focused.

Rule #7: Create a brand. Your brand should conform to your mission--your values and vision for your business. If you stick to this, your brand will stand the test of time. Everything you do should be in alignment with your brand image.

Rule #8: Know your Mission and Vision. The words mission and vision are often used interchangeably, but there's a distinct difference, though they can overlap.

Your business's mission reflects the business's current objectives. But mission can refer to small objectives or tasks for your weekly agenda or larger long term goals for the business.

Your vision for the business defines how you see its future--what you want your business to represent--the values you've instilled and how they inform all your business decisions. It explains what the business is working towards and what you wish to achieve.

It is essential to be as intentional and as detailed as possible with these statements. Don't copy from Google or someone else's business.

Rule #9: Take advantage of the right resources to vitalize your business. Vitalization projects the desire of every entrepreneur, which is to grow and make money. The four key areas to be focused on to maximize the business's success potential include internet, competition domination, marketing, and heading/leading/managing your business.

Rule #10: Communicate effectively. This extends to all aspects of the business: employee relationships, interaction with vendors, resources, and the public, networking, finding mentorship, and branding.

Rule #11: Remember that everything is a reflection of your management and leadership style. In your entrepreneurship journey, you need to embrace management through leadership. You must intentionally manage your workers and embrace the soft skills needed to manage the business effectively.

Be ambitious, tenacious, self-confident, and self-aware. Sleep on every decision or idea.

Rule #12: Hone your emotional intelligence. The need for emotional intelligence among leaders and entrepreneurs is often pushed under the carpet.

Emotions are just not discussed in the business world. Unfortunately, because humans are involved and humans are emotional creatures, this is an area you'll need to understand.

Many entrepreneurs are unaware of how much self-awareness and self-confidence go in dealing with social interactions.

As a boss, you need to be in tune with your own feelings and emotions without letting them influence business decisions. Don't let emotions like insecurity, anger, or narrowmindedness skew employee relationships. You can't and shouldn't take necessary risks until you are in full control of your emotions.

Rule #13: Invest in knowledge. Invest in staff workshops and seminars if you can afford to. Send your managers to managership training if you can, to help them step up to the job. These things are not a waste because it reflects on their productivity level.

Help them identify their value as individuals. Create a working environment where everyone is eligible to grow. When a bird knows it can be comfortable in an environment, it will not be afraid to fly. Adapt this technique with your workers.

Rule #14: Think of your employees as builders. They will join you to build the business to what you want, so you have to employ people who share similar objectives with yours, people who understand and embrace your vision. Use your instincts to choose people whose vibes resonate with you.

Rule #15: Embrace your team. Establishing a good relationship with your staff should also be among your business priorities. It is common knowledge that teamwork is best. Make your workers feel involved in the activities of the business. You will be shocked at how much good vibes this will bring to your workplace and positively affect productivity.

While doing all this ensures balance, don't forget to enforce the much-needed discipline around the workplace. Avoid mixing business with pleasure. Ensure that work ethics are respected and advocate for mutual respect amongst workers.

Rule #16: Learn to maximize resources. Money is usually a sensitive topic, and it honestly does not have to be.

Work to stay on top of your business's monetary affairs so you can achieve financial freedom. Gain the basic knowledge needed to properly handle finances: accounts, payroll, expenses, costs, profit, margins... all of it.

Acquaint yourself with every financial detail of your business. Your goal is to make money--profit--so as soon as you notice a problem that you aren't knowledgable enough to handle, seek the help and guidance of business finance professionals.

Rule #17: Know your market. do your homework by conducting an in-depth analysis of the demographic of your target market: their spending habits, disposable income, where and how they shop, and so on.

Rule #18: Make customer service a priority. I saved this for last because this is a crucial part of running a business. You might provide excellent service or sell a worthy product, but how is your customer service?

You should have adequate staff to deal with customers; you need to be ready to step into action when things go wrong. Your product or service might not be their best option, but your customer service can win them over.

With all these tips and tricks, I am confident that if you are diligent then you will be ready to take on the business world.

Some of you might feel the entrepreneurship journey is not for you, that it's just too much work, or that you'll need to change who you are. That is okay and no one will think less of you for being able to be that self-aware.

For those who will press on: You cannot embody all the needed traits all at once, but you can work toward them. Some will come naturally to you; others you will need to commit to learning. You do not have to be 100% all once, but you must strive to be better than yesterday continually.

Embrace your advancements. Even very small steps that are successfully implemented are to your credit. I say this because you might continuously doubt yourself, which might prevent you from making serious moves or might cause you to make the wrong move, but do not hold back.

Do not let fear keep you from attaining your dream. Be flexible in your decisions because the only constant thing in life is change, and for you to adapt to change quickly, you have to be flexible.

Do not only focus on improving yourself but those that work for you too.

With your knowledge of these facts and details, I believe in you. You have all it takes to succeed in any industry you set your mind to. Good luck, today's explorers and budding leaders of tomorrow!

Go and conquer!

Leaderpreneur takes a comprehensive look at the steps needed to create a successful startup business in any field, gain the loyalty and respect of employees, and survive changes in the market or your industry.

Aaron gives you all the fundamentals from screening & hiring to weeding out ineffective people, leadership, team building and relationship skills, finances, budgeting, planning, growth or scaling, and dealing with challenges and obstacles.

Learn what it takes to be an organizer, leader, and entrepreneur in your own right, how to gain the trust of your team so everyone is a valued asset to the company, and how to avoid the pitfalls that cause a great percentage of startups to fail in the first five years.

If you want to begin a business of your own, *Leaderpreneur* is the place to start.

By learning the methods and approaches presented here--methods that have been honed by decades of successful leaders and entrepreneurs--your chances of survival in the cutthroat world of business stands a greater than average chance of not only surviving but flourishing through profit, growth and effective leadership.

www.ingramcontent.com/pod-product-compliance
Lightning Source LLC
Chambersburg PA
CBHW070903080526
44589CB00013B/1166